Open for Debate

Patients' Rights

KEEP PATIENTS FIRS

SAVE OUR HEAL

Open for Debate

Patients' Rights

Corinne J. Naden

mc Marshall Cavendish
Benchmark
New York

Many thanks to Fran Kelly and Pam Cardozo,
Sleepy Hollow, New York, for their helpful suggestions
and expertise. Thanks to Henry T. "Hank" Greely,
Deane F. and Kate Edelman Johnson Professor of Law,
Stanford Law School, for his thoughtful
review of the manuscript.

Marshall Cavendish Benchmark
99 White Plains Road
Tarrytown, NY 10591
www.marshallcavendish.us
Copyright © 2008 by Marshall Cavendish Corporation

Library of Congress Cataloging-in-Publication Data
Naden, Corinne J.
Patients' rights / by Corinne Naden.
p. cm.— (Open for debate)
Summary: "Discusses patients' rights, including the issues surrounding
physician-assisted suicide, HMOs, the rights of children, abortion, stem
cell research, and the difference between public and private
rights"—Provided by publisher.
Includes bibliographical references and index.
ISBN-13: 978-0-7614-2576-2
1. Medical policy—United States—Juvenile literature. I. Title.
RA395.A3.N286 2006
362.10973—dc22 2006021786

Photo research by Lindsay Aveilhe and Linda Sykes/
Linda Sykes Picture Research, Inc., Hilton Head, SC

All photographs copyright © AP/Wide World Photos, Inc.

Publisher: Michelle Bisson
Art Director: Anahid Hamparian
Series Designer: Sonia Chaghatzbanian

Printed in China

1 3 5 6 4 2

Contents

KEEP PATIENTS FIRS

SAVE OUR HEAL

KEEP PATIENTS FIRST
SAVE OUR HEALTH

Keep Patients First — Save our Health Coalition of health care advocates, hospitals, nursing homes, labor unions, religious, seniors, and children's organizations who care about health care

In 1973, the American Hospital Association adopted
a Patient's Bill of Rights. It was revised in October 1992
and again in December 2003. It lists fifteen patients'
rights, among them the right to considerate and respectful
care and the right to privacy. The aim of the document is
to encourage all hospitals and health care institutions in
the United States to support those rights in the interests of
delivering the best patient care.

In 1996, Congress passed the Health Insurance Portability and Accountability Act (HIPAA). It ensures the
privacy and confidentiality of patient information; it protects patient information; and it sets uniform electronic
transaction standards. It is a federal law. It affects everyone who works in a hospital and associated clinics. The
hospital may be subject to fines and even criminal action if
it ignores the HIPAA. The hospital is directed to take disci-
plinary action against any hospital employee who violates
the HIPAA. It also lists patient's rights for those who are
speech-and hearing-impaired.

An example of the HIPAA statement is from Phelps
Memorial Hospital Center, a 235-bed facility in Sleepy
Hollow, New York. It is typical of such statements in hos-
pitals all over the country.

Patients' rights statements differ somewhat from state
to state. There are also patients' bills of rights for nursing
homes, and they differ from the hospital bill of rights.

Does the Patients' Bill of Rights really protect patients?
Most people are unaware that there is such a statement.
They go to a doctor or a hospital if they must and expect

to be treated well and fairly. But few know enough to demand certain treatments for themselves or loved ones.

What about other rights, inside or outside the hospital? Does a person have the right to refuse life-prolonging treatment in case of severe, incapacitating illness? The answer might seem to be a simple yes. But what if that person could not speak for himself or herself? What if that person's wishes were not written down? Who gets to decide?

Does a person have the right to expect a valid prescription medicine to be filled by the pharmacist? The answer seems obvious. But what if the pharmacist's religious or other beliefs make him or her refuse to fill the prescription? Whose rights take over in that case?

A person is in extreme pain from a fatal illness and asks a doctor to assist in his or her suicide. The doctor agrees. Does the patient have that right? Does the doctor?

The U.S. health care system has sought ways to protect the rights of those who use it. But with rights come responsibilities. Along with the fifteen patients' rights listed in the document are eight responsibilities of patients.

Patients in the U.S. health care system have a responsibility to:

1. **Provide data about past illnesses, medications, and hospital stays.**
2. **Make sure they understand the illness and proposed treatment.**
3. **Give the hospital or other facility a copy of their advance directive if they have one.**
4. **Tell their doctors or other health care workers if they have trouble following the prescribed treatment.**
5. **Be aware of hospital rules and regulations and the reasons for them.**

6. Provide necessary data for insurance claims.

7. Be considerate of hospital staff and other patients.

8. Realize that their health care is also up to them.

In other words, the ways in which patients follow doctors' orders during the course of an illness may have a huge impact on the outcome.

This book explores the many different aspects of patients' rights and responsibilities and the possible conflicts that may occur when a health crisis develops. Being prepared does not always answer all the questions. But the very worst time to question a patient's rights is when you are faced with quick decisions about your own health or the health of someone for whom you are legally responsible.

1

Who Has the Right to Die?

Does a person have the right to decide that he or she wants to die? The quick answer is yes and no. A competent person has the legal right to refuse medical care even if the refusal may cause death. A competent person has the legal right to refuse medical care even if his or her family objects.

A competent person also has the right to draw up an advance directive, or living will. It is a document that goes into effect when a living person is judged incompetent and cannot speak for himself or herself concerning medical treatment. It is different than a last will and testament, which generally lists money and possessions to be left to individuals upon a person's death. All U.S. states honor living wills, although there are differences in their makeup and application from state to state. And although they are legal, not all hospitals honor living wills.

Despite their intention, living wills rarely are able to predict exactly the patient's situation. The Durable Power of Attorney for Health Care (DPAHC) better serves the patient because it appoints a surrogate to carry out his or her wishes. The DPAHC can also allow for giving medical advice to the surrogate. In addition, some states have statutes that designate a next of kin to make medical decisions.

A living will or a DPAHC designates a person's wishes only if he or she becomes incompetent—that is, rendered unable, for whatever reason, to make decisions. It details whether a person does or does not want extended medical treatment under any and all circumstances. The living will or the DPAHC may say that no special devices, such as respirators or feeding tubes, should be used in the event of accident or illness. Withholding these devices differs from withdrawing life support, meaning to take away special devices already in place.

The meaningful word in all these cases is *competent*. And from that word follow all the issues that make the right-to-die question not at all easy to answer.

The Right of Refusal

It is generally agreed in the United States that competent people can legally refuse medical care. They may do so for whatever reason. The right to refuse treatment is recognized as part of the common law doctrine of informed consent. Virtually all states recognize it. The doctrine says that a person has the right to obtain information about his or her medical condition and about treatment options, risks, and possible outcomes. With that information, the person can then decide to accept or refuse medical treatment. For minor patients or those judged incompetent, these same rights apply, but they are directed through a surrogate, meaning whoever can legally speak for the patient.

For competent patients, the right-to-die issue is fairly clear, at least where the law is concerned. But it is a far different situation when the patient is not able to speak for himself or herself. Over the past few decades, three cases in particular in the right-to-die debate became major public issues. They all involved young women—Karen Quinlan, Nancy Cruzan, and Terri Schiavo. And each case shows how complicated the matter becomes when the courts and legislators are involved in what starts out as a family problem and tragedy. Although some Supreme Court as well as other rulings have stemmed from these cases, the issue is far from being decided from a legal standpoint.

Karen Quinlan

In April 1975, Karen Ann Quinlan, age twenty-one, collapsed at a party after she had consumed alcohol and a Valium tranquilizer. She was stabilized at the hospital emergency room, but she suffered brain damage. A tube was inserted to give her food and water, and she breathed with the aid of a respirator. The doctors concluded that she was in a permanent coma, today called a persistent vegetative state.

A persistent vegetative state is different from a general coma, which is a deep state of unconsciousness. The person in a coma is alive but cannot respond to anything in the environment. A coma may be caused by a severe head trauma or a complication of illness. It is generally not considered a permanent condition. In a persistent vegetative state, the person has not only lost awareness of the environment but has lost all brain function as well, with the exception of breathing and circulation. The eyes may open in response to stimuli, and patients may even cry or laugh.

Karen's father asked the court to appoint him as her guardian so that he could legally have her respirator unplugged. That would presumably result in her death. But he did not ask that her feeding tube be removed. He was

THE CASE OF KAREN ANN QUINLAN CAST THE RIGHT-TO-DIE
MOVEMENT IN THE PUBLIC EYE IN THE MID-1970S. HER MOTHER,
JULIA QUINLAN, WROTE A MEMOIR CONCERNING THE FAMILY'S
AGONIZING DECISION TO REMOVE THEIR DAUGHTER FROM LIFE
SUPPORT AND FIGHT FOR HER RIGHT TO DIE.

13

merely making the distinction between what he regarded as ordinary and extraordinary means of sustaining life. The request became a much-publicized legal battle, opposed by Karen's doctors, a local lawyer, and the New Jersey state attorney general.

The New Jersey trial court refused Quinlan's request. It said that any decision to change her life support systems was up to the doctors attending her and that they were acting according to recognized medical standards of the time. But the Supreme Court of New Jersey reversed the lower court. It also gave permission for all life support to be withdrawn.

Only the respirator was unplugged, however, in May 1976. Karen lived another ten years in a New Jersey nursing home sustained only by the feeding tube. She died on June 11, 1985. As a result of the Quinlan case, the number of ethics committees grew rapidly throughout the country to debate the issue. However, the nature of the right-to-die debates changed as a result of the New Jersey Supreme Court. The court also ruled that a patient had a right to refuse medical care on the basis of an unstated but constitutional right of privacy.

Nancy Cruzan

Five years later, in 1990, the U.S. Supreme Court made its first decision about the constitutional interests of patients who are dying. The case was *Cruzan* v. *Director, Missouri Department of Health*, argued December 6, 1989. After surviving an automobile accident, Nancy Cruzan was pronounced incompetent as she lay in a Missouri state hospital. She showed no signs of brain function. Her parents asked that her life support system be ended, which would result in her death. The hospital refused. But a state trial court said the termination was legal. A person has the legal right, said the court, to refuse treatment—in this case, her parents had the legal right.

NANCY CRUZAN'S PARENTS TOOK THEIR BATTLE TO REMOVE THEIR DAUGHTER FROM LIFE SUPPORT TO THE U.S. SUPREME COURT IN 1990. THE COURT RULED THAT A PATIENT OR HIS OR HER LEGAL REPRESENTATIVE HAS THE RIGHT TO REFUSE TREATMENT.

The Missouri Supreme Court reversed the lower court. Among other things, it ruled that her parents could not make the choice in the absence of a living will.

The matter went to the U.S. Supreme Court, which ruled on June 25, 1990. By a 5 to 4 margin, the Court agreed with the Missouri Supreme Court. It ruled that individuals can refuse medical treatment under due process, but not in the case of incompetent patients. "Rehnquist's [chief justice at the time] majority opinion ruled both that a state may confine terminal decisions on behalf of incompetent patients to instances when the patient has previously expressed such a preference and that the state may demand clear evidence of the patient's wishes." By agreeing that a patient had a right to refuse medical care, the Court strengthened the due process doctrine, making it a national standard. However, her parents were able to go back to a lower court in Missouri, and this time they won.

Terri Schiavo

By 2003, the nation once again was caught up in the right-to-die issue. This tragedy involved Terri Schiavo, a young woman declared to be in a persistent vegetative state. The focus this time began with who had the right to speak for her.

Married in 1984, Theresa Marie and Michael Schiavo moved two years later from Southampton, Pennsylvania, to St. Petersburg, Florida, where Terri's parents lived. In February 1990, at the age of twenty-seven, Terri Schiavo suffered cardiac arrest. This was thought to be the result of an eating disorder, which caused a potassium imbalance. A lack of potassium in the body can severely affect heart and body functions. A lack of oxygen following the attack resulted in severe brain damage. According to her doctors, her examinations showed that she was in a persistent vegetative state. She had periods of sleep and wakefulness and

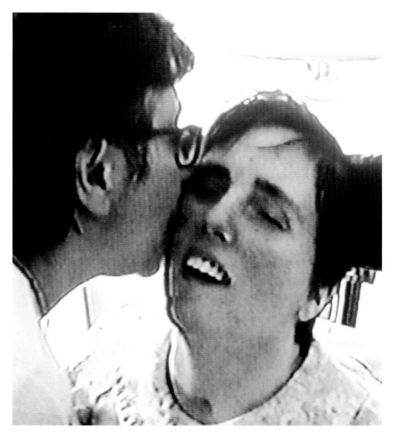

TERRI SCHIAVO WAS IN A PERSISTENT VEGETATIVE STATE FOR FIFTEEN YEARS WHILE HER HUSBAND AND HER PARENTS—AND EVENTUALLY THE NATION, INCLUDING THE PRESIDENT OF THE UNITED STATES—FOUGHT OVER HER RIGHTS, SINCE SCHIAVO COULD NOT SPEAK FOR HERSELF. ON MARCH 18, 2005, HER FEEDING TUBE WAS REMOVED. SHE DIED ON MARCH 31 OF THAT YEAR.

gave some reflex responses to noise or light. However, she showed no signs of emotion, understanding, or physical activity on her own.

This condition would remain virtually unchanged for fifteen years. During that time, Terri's husband and parents fought over her treatment and the nation was drawn into the tragedy. One doctor's analysis was: "Distortion by interest groups, media hyperbole, and manipulative use of videotape characterized this case and demonstrate what can happen when a patient becomes more a precedent-setting symbol than a unique human being."

At Humana Northside Hospital in St. Petersburg, Terri was given a percutaneous endoscopic gastrostomy, or PEG. Tubes were inserted into her body to provide her with food and liquids. She was discharged in May 1990 and sent to a rehabilitation center in College Park. A month later, she was transferred to Bayfront Hospital for more rehabilitation. By this time, her husband had been appointed as her guardian, with no objection from Terri's parents.

Terri's parents and Michael now lived together. They brought Terri home from Bayfront in September, but that lasted only three weeks. The family could not cope with the enormous amount of care that she required.

During the next four years, there were various efforts to rehabilitate Terri. Michael took her to California for experimental brain stimulation. She received continuous speech and occupational therapy at the Sable Palms skilled care facility. But by this time, Michael and Terri's parents were no longer living together, and they argued over her therapy. In 1992, Terri was awarded $250,000 in a malpractice settlement with one of her doctors. An additional one million dollars was later awarded. About three-fourths of the money was put in a trust fund for Terri's treatment. In 1993, her parents demanded that Michael be removed as their daughter's guardian. The court disagreed.

In May 1998, Michael asked the court for permission to remove the PEG tube from his wife. Her parents disagreed. They told the court that their daughter wanted to live. The trial began in January 2000, with Terri's condition unchanged from the initial attack. For the next five years, the question of who had the right to decide the fate of one woman swung back and forth in the courts. The nation's attention became more and more focused on the drama. Initially, the court sided with Michael Schiavo, but petitions from her parents delayed the removal of the tube time and again.

Part of the problem concerned the doctors. Most of those who attended Terri agreed that she was in a persistent vegetative state. However, the doctors chosen by the Schindlers, Terri's parents, often did not. This was complicated by the fact that Terri Schiavo did not have a living will. Although her husband insisted that Terri had told him she did not wish to live in such a condition, there was no legal proof. The newspapers and the public took sides. Michael Schiavo was criticized because by then he was living with another woman whom he met some three years after Terri's collapse. The Schindlers were criticized because they would not accept their daughter's actual condition.

The battle spilled over into the Florida court system. In 2003, Terri's feeding tube was removed for the second time, and the Florida legislature created Terri's Law on October 20. It was passed the next day. It gave Florida governor Jeb Bush the right to call for a one-time stay under special circumstances. The tube was reinserted.

From that day until the spring of 2005, these are the highlights that occurred in the Schiavo right-to-die case:

October 28, 2003: President George W. Bush gets involved as he praises the way his brother handled the Schiavo case.

October 29: Michael Schiavo files court papers declaring Terri's Law unconstitutional.

October 31: Dr. Jay Wolfson is appointed as Terri's guardian.

November 4: Governor Bush asks the circuit court to dismiss Michael Schiavo's suit; the request is denied.

December 1: Wolfson concludes Terri has no chance of improvement.

March 20, 2004: The Catholic Church becomes involved as John Paul II gives an address on life-sustaining treatments and the vegetative state.

May 6: Florida court declares Terri's Law unconstitutional.

July 19: Schindlers file another suit. They charge that withdrawing Terri's tube would violate her ability to exercise her religious beliefs.

August 31: Florida Supreme Court hears arguments over constitutionality of Terri's Law; court declares it unconstitutional.

January 24, 2005: U.S. Supreme Court refuses to review the case.

February 18: Schindlers petition Florida court against removal of the tube.

February 22: Judge stays removal.

February 26: Vatican Radio makes an announcement against removing the tube.

March 2: David Weldon, U.S. representative from Florida, introduces a bill in the House entitled the Incapacitated Persons Legal Protection Act. House passes it on March 16. The bill would allow a federal court to review such cases.

March 17: Schindlers petition U.S. Supreme Court to hear their case. The petition is denied.

On the afternoon of March 8, 2005, after all the appeals and denials and accusations, after all the court decisions, intervention by the governor, and comments by the president and the pope, the PEG tube was removed for the third time from the body of Terri Schiavo. She died on March 31 at 9:05 a.m. This was the same date in 1976 that the New Jersey Supreme Court ruled Karen Quinlan should be disconnected from her respirator.

In those thirteen days between the removal of the tube and Terri's death, there were many petitions to the court to reinsert the tube. The governor asked that the tube be reinserted and another petition went to the U.S. Supreme Court, which again refused to review the case. By May 17, 2005, the last of the protestors, calling for the reinsertion of the tube, slowly filed away from the hospice where Terri Schiavo spent her last months.

An autopsy was performed. The findings generally backed Michael Schiavo's argument that his wife was unaware of her surroundings and could not recover. The report concluded that Terri's brain had shrunk to about half its normal size since her collapse. "This damage was irreversible," Dr. Thogmartin said. "No amount of therapy or treatment would have regenerated the massive loss of neurons." The autopsy also disproved the Schindlers' oft-repeated charge that Michael Schiavo abused their daughter in order to hasten her death.

What the autopsy did not show, however, was what actually caused Terri's collapse in the first place. "Whatever the cause," said Dr. Michael Baden, a forensic pathologist, "it was a natural one rather than a suspicious one."

In March 2006, Michael Schiavo appeared in a TV interview with the *Today* show's Matt Lauer. It was Michael's first television appearance since Terri's death. Schiavo spoke of his book, *Terri: The Truth*, which he said tells what actually took place through the entire ordeal. He was firm during the interview in his declaration that Terri told him she would not want to live in a vegetative state. The day following the publication of Schiavo's book, Terri's parents published their own book on their ordeal.

Religious Protests

Many religious leaders agreed with Terri's parents. Most vocal was the Catholic Church. On March 20, 2004, Pope John Paul II commented indirectly on the Schiavo case. He said there was a "moral obligation" to give food and water to a person in a vegetative state. Reasoned the pope, "the sick person, in a vegetative state, awaiting recovery or his natural end, has the right to basic health care, and to the prevention of complications linked to his state."

Bishop Rene Henry Gracida, Bishop Emeritus of Corpus Christi, Texas, was even more specific in his explanation of church teaching on the subject: "If a person supports euthanasia and assisted-suicide through the illicit rejection or removal of a feeding tube, they are not in communication with the Church. They have separated themselves from the Church."

However, the same article acknowledged that some 32 to 48 percent of Catholics who attend mass favor withdrawing a feeding tube in cases of a persistent vegetative state. In addition, a survey showed that about 90 percent of Catholic doctors in the United States agree with such a position.

What Lessons Learned?

What has been learned from the case of Terri Schiavo and similar cases over the years? Has anything changed?

In 1976, after Quinlan's death, the state of California adopted its first living will law. In 1980, a New York court decided that the tubes should be removed from an eighty-three-year-old monk who was in a persistent vegetative state. He had stated to a number of people—but had never written down—that he did not want to be sustained on life support. It seems clear that in cases where there is no doubt that a person has made clear his or her wishes on the right to die—even if they are verbal—they will generally be honored by the courts, although not necessarily by hospitals.

In November 1990, after Cruzan's death, Congress passed the Patient Self-Determination Act (PSDA). It requires many Medicare and Medicaid providers to inform the patient of certain rights at his or her admission. These include the right to participate in health care decisions and the right to accept or refuse treatment.

It is clear that a vast majority of the American people do not want lawmakers interfering in these matters. Shortly after Terri Schiavo's death, a CBS poll indicated that 82 percent of Americans were against the interference of Congress in the case. Lawmakers on either side of the question made no comment.

The Incapacitated Persons Legal Protection Act was introduced in the House in 2005. Shortly after, a similar bill was introduced in the Senate. No law has yet come from either bill.

The right-to-die issue is legally settled in the United States, at least for those who are competent or those who have made their wishes known before they became incompetent. Four basic documents can generally avoid most problems: (1) a will that indicates who receives certain assets; (2) a financial power of attorney to control the money

Solving End-of-Life Conflicts

Montefiore Medical Center in the Bronx, New York, has a team of doctors and other scientific personnel to help solve the many conflicts that may occur in an end-of-life crisis. The group hears about 100 cases a year, and it has been closely watched since the long debate over Terri Schiavo. After studying a patient, the group meets with spouses or other relatives. The medical condition is discussed as well as the known wishes of both the patient and relatives. The idea is to avoid the long, drawn-out confrontations that may occur among family members in a time of crisis. Straight talk and understanding are the tools that the group uses.

and assets of the incapacitated person; (3) a living will outlining what medical treatments are acceptable; and (4) a health care surrogate to talk to doctors and other medical personnel in place of the incapacitated patient, although this is not accepted in all medical institutions.

Most teenagers think of living wills and other medical directives—if they think of them at all—as strictly the concern of senior citizens. But accidents and strange circumstances do happen. Anyone coming of age might seriously consider the right and responsibility of expressing his or her medical wishes. If Karen Quinlan, Nancy Cruzan, and Terry Schiavo had signed living wills, despite their youth, the fight over their right to die might never have existed. Teenagers might also be interested enough to find out if parents and other family members have signed their own medical directives for the future.

2
Physician-Assisted Suicide

The right-to-die issue leads to an end-of-life issue. Or, put another way, if a person seriously wishes to die, does that person have the right to ask a doctor for help in doing so? And does the doctor have the right to say yes? There are heated arguments on both sides of this question, which is known as physician-assisted suicide.

There is a difference between euthanasia and physician-assisted suicide. Euthanasia, which means *good death* in Greek, is described as painlessly putting to death those who have incurable conditions or diseases. It is sometimes called mercy killing. Giving a drug overdose to bring on death is an example. Most hospital deaths today are the result of a decision to withhold or withdraw support. Sometimes, physicians walk a narrow line between relieving pain and euthanasia when that pain relief is likely to hasten a patient's death.

Although similar to mercy killing, physician-assisted suicide has one big difference. It is the patient, not the doctor, who administers the pill or drug that causes death. At least that was so until the appearance of Jack Kevorkian.

The Life's Work of Dr. Death

Jack Kevorkian, a seventy-eight-year-old retired pathologist, was sentenced to ten to twenty-five years for giving a lethal injection to a dying man. The patient was suffering from amyotrophic lateral sclerosis (ALS). The always fatal condition is also known as Lou Gehrig's disease because the famous first baseman of the New York Yankees died

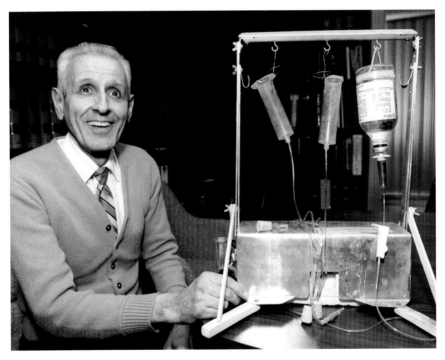

DR. JACK KEVORKIAN'S NAME BECAME SYNONYMOUS WITH ASSISTED SUICIDE IN THE 1980S. HERE HE IS PICTURED WITH HIS SO-CALLED "SUICIDE MACHINE" IN 1991. AT THAT TIME, A MICHIGAN COURT FOUND HIM INNOCENT OF TWO CHARGES OF ASSISTED SUICIDE. HE WAS CONVICTED AND IMPRISONED IN A LATER CASE, BUT IN DECEMBER 2006, HE WAS AWARDED PAROLE IN JUNE 2007.

of it in 1941. ALS weakens and eventually destroys the muscles, rendering the person unable to move and finally unable to breathe. Life expectancy is three to five years after diagnosis.

The case that brought on his jail sentence was not the first time Kevorkian had assisted in a suicide. Nor was it the first time he went to jail for doing so. Through his long struggle to aid those with a terminal illness, Kevorkian earned the title of Dr. Death. He believes that people who suffer from an incurable and painful illness should be allowed to die, if they wish, when and how they choose. His stand has brought him admirers and detractors and, in most cases, trouble with the law. "Many of his critics fear that if Kevorkian has his way, the line between voluntarily ending one's life with a doctor's help and being coerced into 'choosing' suicide . . . will become irrevocably blurred," says H. R. Wilson. But, until late 2006, Kevorkian was unmoved by the critics. In December 2006, it was announced that he would be paroled in June 2007 from his 10-to-25-year sentence when he promised not to assist in any other suicides.

Kevorkian was born in Pontiac, Michigan, in 1928. He went to the University of Michigan, graduating from medical school in 1952. He specialized in pathology, which is the study of diseases and their effect on the body's tissues and fluids. In later years he recalled that during his internship, one of the patients was a woman with cancer who, according to Kevorkian, seemed "as though she was pleading for help and death at the same time." From then on he felt that to assist in a patient's suicide was an ethical practice.

After some time in Korea and conducting research in West Germany, Kevorkian became a resident at Detroit Receiving Hospital. There, in 1956, he began to be called Dr. Death. He took photos of patients' retinas at the time of death for study purposes. Over the next three decades, he became noticed more and more for his writings on physician-assisted suicide and for building devices to aid those who wanted to die. Such a device allows an incapacitated patient to turn off life-support equipment or to lethally inject or gas himself or herself at the touch of a button.

His notoriety led to his first physician-assisted suicide in 1989. Janet Adkins, suffering from Alzheimer's disease, which destroys mental ability, contacted him. She died in June the following year by pushing the button on the machine Kevorkian invented. It injected lethal fluid into her veins. With each case, the controversy grew. After his third physician-assisted suicide in 1991, Michigan revoked his license. With questions about his methods, in 1993 Michigan passed a law banning assisted suicide. That year, Kevorkian was arrested twice on charges of aiding the death of a thirty-year-old victim of ALS. Kevorkian freely admitted his participation and was acquitted at a trial in early 1994.

Over the next few years, Kevorkian continued his crusade. However, in 1998, circumstances changed when he admitted to being a *direct* participant in the death of a patient. In other words, it was Kevorkian himself who administered the lethal dose, not the dying patient. He was charged with performing active euthanasia.

In November 1998, Kevorkian appeared on the television program *60 Minutes*. He brought a videotape with him. It showed him administering a lethal dose to Thomas Youk, who had ALS. Kevorkian had earlier been contacted by Youk's brother and was asked to administer the dose. Kevorkian said he first tried to convince Youk to carry out the suicide only with his assistance, but in the end he did it himself. He said that he videotaped the procedure and had it aired in order to advance his right-to-die cause. Then, Kevorkian challenged the courts to convict him.

The Michigan court did convict Jack Kevorkian in

1999 of second degree murder and delivery of a controlled substance. He has appealed his conviction but is at present still serving his sentence.

Kevorkian may be the most well-known proponent of physician-assisted suicide, but he is not the only one. In 1991, Dr. Timothy E. Quill, professor of medicine at the University of Rochester, was called to testify before the New York State medical board of inquiry. He had written an article in the *New England Journal of Medicine* describing how he prescribed a lethal dose of barbiturates for a patient suffering from acute leukemia, knowing she intended to commit suicide. After listening to testimony, the board decided not to revoke his medical license.

The Medical World's View

When former Vermont governor Howard Dean entered the democratic presidential nomination race in 2004, he spoke of his medical experience. He earned his medical degree from Albert Einstein College of Medicine in New York in 1978. During the campaign for the Democratic party nomination, which he lost to Democratic candidate John Kerry, he supported physician-assisted suicide and euthanasia. Said Dean, "I as a physician would not be comfortable administering lethal drugs, but I think this is a very private, personal decision. . . . I am very amused by the Right Wing . . . who talk about liberty but then decide they're going to scrutinize everyone's behavior and tell them what they can and cannot do. There can't be a much more personal decision an individual makes than how to die."

Kerry favored assisted suicide but admitted that it made him uncomfortable. The issue was not a deciding one in his victory over Dean.

Dean's support for physician-assisted suicide puts him very much at odds with medical organizations. By a large margin, the American Medical Association, as well as many similar organizations worldwide, are opposed. According to surveys, more than half of U.S. doctors and about two-thirds of the public now support physician-assisted suicide. That puts the doctors at odds with their own organizations.

Paramount in the opposition by medical associations is the Hippocratic oath, which most physicians take. Attributed to the ancient Greek physician Hippocrates, the oath is generally adopted as a guide for the medical profession. Upon taking the oath, the physician promises to protect the lives of his or her patients and to refrain from causing them harm.

That would prevent the doctor from assisting in a patient's death, says the medical profession in general. Not so, declare Dean and others who support the practice. There is a place, they say, for a humane, caring end to a life lived in unbearable pain and suffering. They point to developments abroad as well as in the United States that indicate change is coming.

Where Are We Heading?
The Groningen Protocol

In October 2004, a hospital in the Netherlands made a startling proposal—the first of its kind—regarding the use of euthanasia. Called the Groningen Protocol, it stated that a committee of doctors had been formed to decide the fate of newborns or infants suffering from painful, incurable diseases as well as other severely handicapped or disabled persons. "Under the Groningen Protocol, if doctors at the hospital think a child is suffering unbearably from a terminal condition, they have the authority to end the child's life." Furthermore, said the Protocol, the committee's decision, not the parents, would be final. The wishes of the parents would be taken into consideration, but the authorization would come from the doctors, with or without parental consent.

Under the protocol, deaths by euthanasia are not reported to the coroner. Instead, doctors report to a review committee composed of a physician, lawyer, and ethicist. A prosecutor does not become involved unless the panel determines that the death aid was inappropriate. Those in favor of this new approach believe that hidden euthanasia instances will now be out in the open.

The Groningen Protocol marks the first time that any nation has legalized mercy killings of terminally ill patients, in this case patients as old as twelve years. It "topples a barrier that has stood intact even in the permissive Netherlands," said one dissenter.

To some, this development is an example of appalling brutality. To others, it may relieve the appalling suffering of some infants and children. Those in the middle question whether this opening of a door will lead to other actions in the longstanding debate over right-to-die, euthanasia, and mercy-killing issues. They ask: Where are we heading?

Physician-Assisted Suicide in Oregon

In 1991, the state of Washington attempted to legalize physician-assisted suicide, followed by the state of California the following year. Both attempts were voted down. That seems inconsistent with the surveys that say Americans, by a large margin, favor such a procedure.

In 1994, Oregon voters narrowly passed a bill legalizing physician-assisted suicide—called the Death with Dignity Act. It passed by a margin of 52 to 48 percent. In 1997, the Oregon legislature asked voters to repeal the law. That request was rejected—51 to 49 percent.

The Death with Dignity Act allows doctors in Oregon to give lethal medication to those who are terminally ill. It does, however, have a number of procedures that must be followed. The patient's doctor as well as another physician must confirm that the patient has less than six months to

OREGON REMAINS THE ONLY STATE THAT ALLOWS PHYSICIAN-ASSISTED SUICIDE. IN 2001, THE FEDERAL GOVERNMENT CHALLENGED THAT LAW. OREGON CHALLENGED THE GOVERNMENT. THE CASE WENT TO THE U.S. SUPREME COURT. IN 2005, THOSE IN FAVOR OF THE LAW DEMONSTRATED IN FRONT OF THE SUPREME COURT BUILDING. THE JUSTICES RULED IN FAVOR OF THE OREGON LAW IN JANUARY 2006.

live. The doctors must judge that the patient is competent to make such a request. The patient must be informed of all alternatives. The request for physician-assisted suicide must be in writing. In addition, the patient has to make two oral requests for the procedure, at least fifteen days apart. The prescription that the doctor writes for lethal medication must be sent to the Oregon Health Division. The patient self-administers the medication whether or not the doctor is present.

The first suicide under the act was reported in March 1998. By the end of the year, physician-assisted suicide was included in the Oregon Health Plan. Blue Cross and Blue Shield medical plans now cover such suicides in the state. Contrary to the fears of those who are against the Death with Dignity Act, there has not been a rush of such cases in Oregon since its inception. From 1998 until 2005, 246 people used the act to bring about their deaths. In 2005, of the roughly 40,000 people who died in Oregon, 38 used the Death with Dignity Act.

Action against the Death with Dignity Act came from the federal government in 2001. John Ashcroft, attorney general at that time, declared that any doctor who prescribed lethal medication would be prosecuted under the U.S. Controlled Substances Act (CSA). The CSA is the legal foundation for the government's fight against drugs and their abuse. It lists drugs according to their use and potential for harm.

Oregon reacted to Ashcroft's declaration by suing the federal government. The state won when the Ninth Circuit Court ruled in its favor. The matter went to the U.S. Supreme Court.

In January 2006, the decision of the Court was released. The Supreme Court declared that Ashcroft was wrong. In a 6 to 3 ruling, it said that the attorney general acted without legal authority. This high profile case was thought by some to open the door for similar legislation in other states. Proponents of physician-assisted suicide think that is where we are heading. It should be noted, however, that the high Court did not say that Oregon's Death with Dignity Act was legal; it said only that Ashcroft's declaration was not.

3

When Rights Conflict

Sometimes patients' rights run into conflict with the rights of people in the medical industry who hold different religious or moral beliefs. Sometimes patients' rights are compromised by the goals or marketing techniques of drug companies who sell medications. Sometimes a patient suffers the ultimate violation of rights because a doctor or other health care provider was careless or unqualified and caused injury or even death.

When Patients and Pharmacists Disagree

A rape victim in Texas walked into a pharmacy with a valid prescription for emergency contraception, often called the morning-after pill. The pharmacist refused to fill it. He said he was objecting on personal moral grounds. The *New England Journal of Medicine* told of a pharmacist in New Hampshire who would not fill a patron's prescription for emergency contraception. Instead, said the article, "he berated a twenty-one-year-old single mother, who then, in her words, 'pulled the car over in the parking lot and just cried.'"

Who has the right here: the person who needs and wants the medication and has a valid prescription or the pharmacist who can provide it but refuses to do so on personal, moral, or religious grounds? The answer is no one knows, although the backers of conscientious objection seem to be in the wining seat so far. The outcome remains unclear.

At present, nearly all states have some kind of legal protection for health care workers who are against providing reproductive services, such as the morning-after pill. Four states—Arkansas, Mississippi, Georgia, and South Dakota—fully protect those pharmacists who refuse to fill such prescriptions. In North Carolina, pharmacists can refuse to fill contraception prescriptions, but they must direct patients to a pharmacy that will fill them. California, Missouri, and New Jersey, in contrast, all have bills in the process that tell pharmacists to fill any valid prescription.

In other states, different tugs-of-war are being waged. For instance, in 2005, a pharmacist in Chicago refused to fill two prescriptions for the morning-after pill. State governor Rod Blagojevich reacted by sending out an emergency order that told all state pharmacies to fill such prescriptions. That led three pharmacists to file a suit. They said their moral and religious convictions were being violated. In turn, the governor is trying to have his order made into law.

The list of pharmacists who are refusing to dispense birth control medicine on moral grounds is growing, but so is the opposition. The battle has led lawmakers in Washington to propose a bill making it illegal not to give a patient any legally asked-for medication.

In 2004, the Food and Drug Administration (FDA) refused to grant over-the-counter status to emergency contraceptives. Over-the-counter status would have meant that the patient could bypass the pharmacist, thus averting one potential problem. In six states, pharmacists can give contraceptive medication without a prescription. However, in August 2006, the FDA did approve the over-the-counter sale of emergency contraceptives to women age eighteen and older. They do not have to first see a doctor. Younger teenagers still need a prescription.

The battle lines are drawn on the pharmacist conscientious objection issue. Here are the two sides. A pharmacist has the right to object to fill a prescription because:

1. Other U.S. medical professionals can act according to their beliefs. Doctors and nurses don't have to perform abortions if they don't want to. A doctor can treat any patient he or she wants to, except in an emergency room.

2. A democratic society allows its citizens to refuse to take part in an act that is contrary to their personal beliefs. During World War II, for instance, men who were against war on religious grounds, such as the Quakers, were called conscientious objectors. Instead of being inducted into the army, they were allowed to perform other duties.

On the other side, a pharmacist does not have the right to object to fill a prescription because:

1. As a member of the medical profession, the pharmacist, like other medical providers, is expected to place the patient's health above personal convictions. The patient's health should come first. Objections to providing services can significantly affect a person's health.

2. The right to refuse medication can lead to discrimination. What if a pharmacist realizes a patient has the HIV virus because of the medication he or she is taking? Can that not lead to a refusal to fill the prescription just because the pharmacist is against those with the disease?

3. Most objections to contraceptive medications are based on antiabortion beliefs. But these medications are not abortion pills. For instance, they do not affect a pregnancy already in progress. They are used to prevent one from occurring. In any case, abortion is legal in the United States.

Friend or Foe: The Pharmaceutical Industry

U.S. drug companies are a vital part of the U.S. health care system. The drugs they develop and manufacture save millions of lives and help millions of people to live healthier and longer lives. Drug companies have brought major advances to medicine. In general, most U.S. pharmaceutical houses maintain rigorous scientific standards.

Those issues are rarely disputed by the public. Criticism of the drug industry rests mainly in one area: the astronomical and constantly rising costs of drugs. Says Dr. Jeanne Kassler in her book *Bitter Medicine*:

Drug manufacturers have argued that they should be paid handsomely because their drugs save money by lowering nonmedication costs of disease, such as eliminating surgery or helping people return to work quickly. . . . Although there is no question that the pharmaceutical industry has greatly improved medical care, drug prices have

become a source of contention. As overall medical costs rise, as more people take more medications for more illnesses, as one of the nation's most profitable industries receives extensive tax benefits, the pricing of drugs comes under increasing scrutiny by consumers, insurers, and health-care reformers.

Drug companies respond to such criticism by citing the incredibly high costs of developing new—mainly anti-cancer—and effective drugs. They point out that developing any drug is a highly expensive operation. It may take years of experimentation and trial before a drug is allowed on the market; even after years of trial and error, some never make it.

In addition to pricing, and despite the overall high performance of the drug industry, sometimes questionable marketing practices place a large segment of the population in jeopardy. The rights of patients to receive fair and honest medical treatment are compromised by what many have called unethical and unconscionable practices.

A case in point is Merck & Co. and its marketing of the drug called Vioxx. In 1999, the drug was put on the market for the treatment of arthritis. Vioxx is in a class of painkillers known as COX-2 inhibitors, which also includes Celebrex, marketed by Pfizer and introduced shortly before Vioxx. These drugs claim to solve the problem of patients with arthritis and other ailments that cause chronic pain; namely, taking pain remedies on a daily basis can cause stomach bleeding. The stomach has two enzymes, COX-1 and COX-2, that regulate acid production. COX-2 is called the bad enzyme, which causes bleeding. Vioxx and Celebrex claim to block this bad enzyme and leave the other—good—one.

Within a short time after it was introduced, Vioxx was at the top of the drug sales chart. It was prescribed for

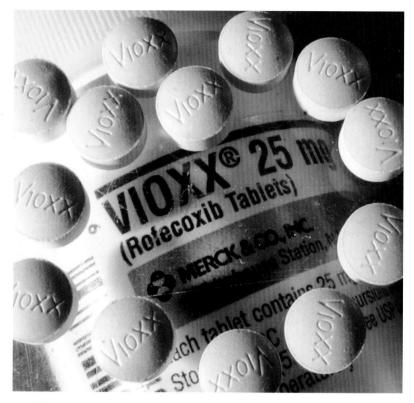

VIOXX WAS A TOP-SELLING ARTHRITIS DRUG UNTIL IT WAS PULLED OFF THE MARKET BY ITS PRODUCER, MERCK & CO., BECAUSE A THREE-YEAR STUDY SHOWED AN INCREASE OF HEART ATTACKS IN THOSE TAKING THE MEDICATION. SINCE THEN, THE COMPANY HAS BEEN EMBROILED IN LAWSUITS.

more than 10 million patients just in the United States. It was marketed in 80 countries and used by more than 80 million people worldwide.

Then came the shocker. Merck suddenly pulled Vioxx off the market on September 30, 2004. The reason was the results of a three-year study involving some 2,600 patients. It showed that there was an increased risk of heart attacks and strokes some eighteen months after patients began taking Vioxx. In fact, the study found there were five times as many heart attacks in those who took Vioxx compared with those who took naproxen, another painkiller. Merck said they were taking action "because we believe it best serves the interests of patients."

A congressional investigation followed. A House committee said that two years after the drug was introduced, an FDA advisory group suggested that evidence pointed to a new clinical trial for Vioxx. Instead, Merck spent some $100 million on a media campaign to assure the public that the drug was safe. The House committee also said that Merck trained its sales staff not to mention the heart attack warnings when they introduced the drug to doctors. Apparently, doctors wrote millions of Vioxx prescriptions without knowing of a possible increased danger of heart problems.

Merck said its marketing practices were fair. The company insisted that doctors had the opportunity to read the study that raised questions about health problems with Vioxx.

As a result of the study and the withdrawal of Vioxx, the FDA announced that it would closely monitor all drugs in that class for similar effects. It called for the withdrawal of Bextra, another COX-2 inhibitor, but not Celebrex, which is still on the market.

The first lawsuit filed against Vioxx was decided on August 19, 2005. Merck was ordered to pay $253 million to the widow of Robert Ernst, a fifty-nine-year-old Wal-Mart employee who took Vioxx and died of a heart attack. Three months later, a New Jersey state court sided with the drug company in *Humeston* v. *Merck*, and in December of that year, a Texas jury failed to return a verdict in *Plunkett* v. *Merck*. The case is to be retried. Also in December, the *New England Journal of Medicine* published an editorial that said Merck deliberately withheld information about the drug, a charge that Merck denies. However, it is true that Merck did not include a warning about

Merck Wins Lawsuit

There are currently about 16,000 lawsuits against Merck for its painkiller Vioxx. One of them was decided in Merck's favor on July 13, 2006. The jury decided that Vioxx did not cause the heart attack suffered by Elaine Doherty, sixty-eight, of New Jersey. Although Merck did not warn Doherty about the cardiac risks, the jury found that the company did properly warn her doctors.

possible heart problems with the drug until 2002. Merck is currently involved in personal injury lawsuits related to Vioxx that may run into the billions of dollars.

The controversy over the drug was not only damaging to the drug industry, which justifiably prides itself on first-class treatment for patients, but it was damaging to the takers of Vioxx and causes concerns for all those who take medications for whatever reasons.

Where do patients' rights come into the drug picture? In general, patients must rely upon the advice and knowledge of their doctors or other health care providers regarding their medications. In the case of Vioxx, those taking the drug were advised to call their doctors immediately about discontinuing the medication. Merck set up a hotline to call for information, and it assured all Vioxx patients that they would be reimbursed for the unused portions of the drug.

Where drugs are concerned, the best way to protect the rights of patients is for each person to be his or her own watchdog. Talk about medications with your doctor, including any possible and risky side effects. Understand what medications you are taking and why. An informed consumer may be a healthier consumer as well.

Patients' Rights in Clinical Trials?

A clinical trial is a research study. It involves human volunteers who have specific health problems. In such a trial, a proposed drug or therapy can be examined under controlled conditions to find out if it is safe and effective in treating the medical condition. Although most studies are conducted with sound medical treatment and intentions, sometimes drug companies can take advantage of the helplessness of people suffering painful and often fatal diseases.

A clinical trial was conducted by Amgen, the world's

largest biotechnology company, with a drug known as GDNF (for glial cell line-derived neurotrophic factor) for the treatment of Parkinson's disease. About four dozen people who suffered from the disease were involved in the study. In September 2004, Amgen stopped the drug, saying it might be dangerous and had proved to be no better than the placebo, or fake drug, given to some.

In April 2005, two of the patients in the trial filed a lawsuit. They requested that Amgen be ordered to continue to give them the drug because it improved their condition. In June, a federal judge denied the request. He said the company did not have a contract to continue to supply the drug and the patients did not have the right to demand that it do so.

The most well-known case of patients' rights abuse in trials was the Tuskegee syphilis study in Macon County, Alabama, between 1932 and 1972. It is often cited as the outstanding example of medical research gone wrong. The U.S. Public Health Service wanted to learn more about syphilis, a venereal disease that left untreated results in painful death. In its clinical study, treatment was withheld from a group of poor black men suffering from the disease. The men were told they were being treated for bad blood, a local term used to describe several ailments. The supposedly six-month study lasted forty years, causing needless pain and suffering. Even when penicillin, used to cure syphilis, became available in 1947, the men in the study were not given it. Although all the men freely agreed to join the study, there is no evidence that the researchers told them of the real purpose.

The Fight over Medical Marijuana

Sometimes drugs are not available because someone refuses to fill a prescription. Sometimes they are not available because they are pulled off the market, as with Vioxx. And sometimes they are not available because of a legal fight over their status: illegal recreational drug or essential medicine? Such is the case with medical marijuana.

Marijuana refers to the leaves of the cannabis plant. It has been commonly used throughout the world to relieve pain and other ailments. However, there has long been controversy over its medical effectiveness. The United States banned it in 1937, claiming it had no legitimate medical purpose. Decades later, it became a highly publicized, highly popular, so-called recreational but illegal drug. Smoking its leaves induces a feeling of euphoria.

However, many current medical studies in the United States point to the beneficial effects of so-called medical marijuana to relieve the pain and suffering of cancer and AIDs patients. It is said to be especially beneficial in reducing the nausea and vomiting from chemotherapy. Therefore, some doctors, medical groups, and volunteer organizations, such as the Compassionate Coalition, are calling for the legalization of the drug. They feel that pain sufferers should have the right to treatment when it exists.

In opposition, many experts object to legalizing marijuana for medical use. They say that pills containing THC, the active ingredient in marijuana, produce the same good effects.

What exists today is a fight between the federal government and some state governments over marijuana policy. In June 2005, the U.S. Supreme Court ruled in *Gonzales* v. *Raich* that Congress has the right to outlaw the use of marijuana even in those states where it is legal (Alaska, California, Colorado, Hawaii, Maine, Montana, Nevada, Oregon, Rhode Island, Vermont, and Washington).

The federal government says no to marijuana use because it has no accepted medical use. It is illegal except for use in FDA-approved research programs. The debate goes on over what some consider to be a fight for patients' rights.

Just Sick, Not Criminals

Advocates of medicinal uses for marijuana were disappointed but not desperate after the Supreme Court decision to outlaw its use, even in the eleven states that permit it. Angel McClary Raich, one of the users whose case was before the Court, said: "Just because we lost this little battle does not mean that the war is over. We're just sick. We're not criminals." Raich suffers from several illnesses and believes that the use of marijuana has kept her alive. Another user is Dana May, who describes the pain from his medical condition as "nightmarish." He grew marijuana in his backyard until he was raided by state and federal authorities.

Those who defend the Supreme Court decision say: "We don't want truly sick and dying people to be scammed into thinking they are being medically treated by smoking pot. We believe that people who are truly sick need good, legitimate medicine."

New York Times, June 6, 2005

Medical Malpractice and Medical Injury

Medical malpractice is a term indicating that a medical provider is being sued because a patient has suffered injuries as a result of the provider's negligence. It is frightening—and possibly career-threatening—for the doctor. It is frightening—and possibly life-ending—for the patient.

Nearly 19,000 cases of medical malpractice were reported in the United States in 2005, with about 50 percent of those made against surgeons. Estimates are that more than 50 percent of all U.S. doctors are sued at least once during their working lifetime. Not only has the number of lawsuits increased, so have the payouts by doctors.

The following example is not unusual. A woman may

DOCTORS ARE VERY MUCH AGAINST THE AWARDS GIVEN IN MEDICAL MALPRACTICE SUITS. IN MARCH 2003, DOCTORS WHO SUPPORT CAPS ON MEDICAL MALPRACTICE LAWSUIT AMOUNTS DEMONSTRATED IN TALLAHASSEE, FLORIDA.

have one or two children born naturally, and the second or third by caesarean section. That is an operation in which the baby is taken by cutting through the walls of the stomach and uterus. The name comes from the Roman general Caesar, said to have been born in that manner. It is performed when, for various reasons that would endanger the life of mother or child, the baby cannot be born normally through the vaginal, or birth, canal.

If the woman becomes pregnant again, she may not want another operation. She may decide to have her next child by VBAC (pronounced VEE-back), meaning vaginal birth after caesarean. However, she may be quite shocked to learn from her obstetrician that the choice is not hers. She may be told to have a second caesarean operation. If not, she may have to leave the hospital of her choice and go to another.

Why? Of the approximately half million U.S. births in 2005, one in every four was caesarean. Doctor Joshua A. Copel of Yale University School of Medicine gave one reason for this. "Malpractice, malpractice, malpractice. Not that much has changed about the American population to account for such an increase in Caesarean birth rates except the fear of obstetricians being sued."

To protect against the growth of medical malpractice suits, doctors have to be covered by malpractice insurance, whose premiums are—not surprisingly—also on the rise. For instance, the ProMutual Group, which covers about one-third of licensed doctors in Massachusetts, raised its premium rates more than 12.5 percent in 2002, 20 percent in 2003, and 11 percent in 2004. Doctors in high-risk areas, such as obstetricians, can pay as much as $100,000 a year just for medical malpractice insurance.

Why are malpractice claims on the rise? Are doctors just not as good as they used to be? As it turns out, that is not the case. In general, doctors and other health care professionals are better trained than ever before. New sophisticated technology allows more sophisticated diagnosis and treatment. But it also allows for more mistakes, such as misreading an MRI (magnetic resonance imaging), which takes pictures of the insides of things, including people's stomachs. Also, new technologies allow for the treatment of sicker and older patients, where the risk of complications is greater than the average.

Of greater risk to the patient today than medical malpractice is medical injury. There is a rise in medical injury claims in the United States. Medical injuries may include leaving a clamp or a sponge inside the patient after an operation, or, even more severe, removing the wrong kidney.

What rights and recourse does a patient have in filing a medical malpractice or injury suit? To win a claim, a patient must give evidence that he or she was in the doctor's care and that the doctor's actions were the cause of the injury.

Most malpractice or injury cases are argued before a jury, although in some cases they are decided by a judge only. Usually, a patient has an expert medical witness give testimony at the jury trial. In a case where the wrong kidney was removed, the expert might also be a surgeon who has performed many kidney operations. He or she might explain the correct procedures to follow to avoid such a tragedy as taking out the wrong organ.

In cases of negligence where payment for injury is sought, the patient may use the old rule of *res ipsa loquitor*, which is a Latin phrase meaning "the thing speaks for itself." In other words, it does not have to be explained beyond the obvious facts. An example might be a man who suffered severe back injuries from a malfunctioning store escalator. He sued the company that built and maintained the escalator. The company claimed there was no evidence that it was at fault. However, the court ruled that

The Right to Be Fat?

Everyone knows it's unhealthy to be overweight and even dangerous to be obese. But do you have the right to be fat? A math teacher in Long Island, New York, learned that his extra poundage cost him his job.

Michael D. Frank, 6' 4" and 325 pounds, was fired from the Lawrence Middle School in May 2004. He had taught seventh-grade math there for four years. But after numerous good reports on his work, he was relieved from his duties because the assistant superintendent for curriculum wrote: "You are so big and sloppy" and said that his "obesity was not conducive to learning."

Frank believes he is being discriminated against because of his weight. The case will go to trial.

Newsday, July 7, 2006

the man only had to offer proof that he was injured. The escalator did not work properly; the company was responsible for its working and, therefore, for the man's injury. The thing speaks for itself.

In practice, however, most claims for malpractice or injury do not go to court. In many instances, a doctor's apology (if the injury is not too severe) and an explanation of what occurred will solve the dispute.

When a malpractice claim is warranted, the injured party can file a complaint with various state boards, such as the Board of Medicine for doctors, the Board of Nursing, or the Board of Dentistry. You do not need a lawyer if you file a complaint with one of those boards, but you do need a lawyer if you intend to go to court. Lawyers who specialize in medical malpractice are not always easy to find. The American Civil Liberties Union (ACLU) or state bar associations may be helpful in that area.

4
A Patient's Lack
of Choice

In an ideal world, a patient and his or her doctor sit down and discuss a medical problem. They come to a mutually satisfactory conclusion that is also within the law. But that doesn't always happen. Doctor and patient don't always agree. Either one doesn't always agree with hospital or state rules. Illness may take away a patient's ability to make decisions. And lack of money or social status may also deprive the patient of choices.

A Woman's Choice?

The earlier example concerning a possible medical malpractice suit involving a caesarean birth points out a matter of increasing concern to many American women. Research indicates that the risk of natural birth after a caesarean delivery is greater than once thought. There is fear that an old scar—Caesarean birth is, after all, an operation—will cause a rupture in the wall of the uterus during the birth process. That may very well endanger the mother and result in the death of the baby. Large city hospitals would be prepared to handle such a crisis, but presumably not smaller ones because they do not have sufficient staff on hand. Therefore, many smaller U.S. hospitals are insisting on caesarean birth, taking the choice away from the woman.

Shouldn't a woman have the right to decide on her own method of birth, barring any emergency? Many women and their doctors think so. Dr. Bruce Flamm, an obstetrician with Kaiser Permanente and a professor at the University of California, Irvine, certainly does. He also worries about this trend. "The real issue going across America right now is, what do we do?" he says.

> **Hundreds of thousands of women a year now are coming into hospitals with a previous caesarean, some in communities where every hospital has shut down its VBAC program. That's the issue. Some will go to a lay midwife and have a VBAC in their bedroom. A good number will do fine, but some will have horrendous outcomes.**

Dr. Gerrit Schipper, obstetrics chief at Frederick Memorial Hospital in Frederick, Maryland, once favored the VBAC procedure. Now he doesn't. About 2,000 births take place at his hospital each year. In a three-year period, major problems occurred with three women who were trying normal deliveries after caesareans. Now, the hospital bans VBAC. If one of his patients insists on it, he sends her to a larger hospital in Baltimore, about 60 miles (96 km) away.

There is much debate over this issue. Hospitals say they ban VBAC deliveries to protect the health of the woman. But many women and doctors agree with Dr. Copel. They think the real problem is a hospital's fear of getting sued. In the meantime, the right of a woman to choose her method of birth, barring an emergency or other complication, is—in many parts of the United States—not a choice at all.

Who Needs an Advocate?

Advocacy means the work of an advocate. An advocate is someone who pleads for or defends the cause of another. In the area of patients' rights, advocacy is a concern when a person cannot, for various reasons, make decisions for himself or herself. A minor, of course, cannot legally make certain decisions because of age restrictions; thus the parents, guardians, or court-appointed custodians are the child's advocates. But the advocacy issue is more generally associated with medical conditions.

For example, a daughter may realize that her elderly mother is becoming forgetful and can no longer care for herself. A doctor's examination might determine that the mother is in the early stages of Alzheimer's disease. That is a condition affecting more than four million Americans, most of them elderly. It is the eighth leading cause of death in the United States. "The exact cause of Alzheimer's disease is unknown, but a person's genetic makeup almost certainly plays some role. The disease results in loss of brain cells," write Robert F. Borenstein and Mary A. Languirand.

Early signs of Alzheimer's involve forgetfulness. As the disease progresses, the patient loses the ability to read, write, speak, or understand what someone else is saying. Eventually, even the simplest tasks, such as turning on the TV, are impossible. Complete medical care is necessary in the later stages of Alzehimer's.

Patients with Alzheimer's live an average of eight to ten years after diagnosis, but may live well beyond that. President Ronald Reagan, who left the White House in

1989, disclosed publicly in 1994 that he suffered from the disease. He was rarely seen in public after that and died in 2004 at the age of ninety-three.

It may be necessary at some point to place an Alzheimer's patient in a nursing home. But what happens if a patient with early Alzheimer's will not agree to a nursing home? What if the patient says there is nothing wrong with him or her?

Unless the family is willing to fight the patient through legal channels on this, they must accept his or her decision—as long as the patient is in no immediate danger. But if family members believe the person is a real danger to himself or herself, they may go to the crisis intervention center, or similarly named group, at the local hospital. The family can request a team of medical workers to visit the patient at home. If after the visit the medical team thinks that the patient should be examined further, it has the right to bring him or her into the hospital—even if the patient objects. If all these studies determine that the patient cannot make decisions for himself or herself, the family can take legal steps to declare him or her incompetent.

In the United States, a person is judged to be competent unless proven otherwise. This protects the person, for instance, from those who might want to prove incompetency in order to get his or her money. There must be unbiased, substantial proof that the person is incompetent. That proof would likely come from a medical doctor or psychologist—someone who has nothing to gain by the decision—rather than a family member.

Basically, there are three steps to declare a person incompetent, although they vary somewhat from state to state: (1) a motion is made in court, usually by a family member, for a competency hearing; (2) a court-appointed representative, usually a psychologist, evaluates the competency of the person in question; and (3) a guardian, or advocate, is appointed if the person is judged incompetent. The advocate will make decisions for the person as appropriate and is subject to review by the court at any time.

Is Wealthier Healthier?

The rights of patients in the United States are protected in many ways. A doctor swears to do patients no harm and to treat them fairly and well. A hospital's bill of rights promises the best possible health care and the utmost privacy where possible.

Even so, not everyone in the United States gets the best or even comparable health care. Some of that disparity is due to location. A man in crisis in a small rural town in Mississippi is not likely to get the same prompt, efficient care on the spot that he would in the capital city of Jackson. A woman undergoing delicate cancer surgery at the famed Sloan-Kettering hospital in New York City probably has a better chance of survival and wellness than another woman undergoing the same operation in an-out-of-the way clinic where the operation has rarely been attempted.

Some of the disparity is due to the obvious fact that not all doctors share the same talent and know-how. It is certainly true that the best in medical care can be had in many small, out-of the-way areas in the United States. But it is also true that the larger metropolitan medical institutions generally offer more services and attract the more talented, dedicated doctors who want to work with the latest in medical advances.

So, location may affect your health status, which is a fact most Americans realize. Many also realize another factor—your wealth can affect your health status, too. It is a fact of life that wealthy people can buy better homes and better clothes than poor people, and they also can get better seats in expensive restaurants or box seats at football games. But, more importantly, can people with money get better health care than those without it? The answer, in many instances, seems to be yes.

A prime example in which the wealthy are treated differently is evident in colonoscopy screening. Cancer is the second leading cause of death in the United States. About 570,000 Americans died from the disease in 2005, with colorectal cancer second only to lung cancer in death toll—killing about 57,000 people a year. Most professionals in the medical field agree that a significant portion of colorectal deaths could be eliminated by a single test: the colonoscopy. According to a 2003 study, "Colonoscopy allows doctors to see and remove polyps and cancerous lesions in the colon with great accuracy, and can cut cancer incidence by 60 percent."

The colon, or large bowel, is a hollow tube about five feet long and is the last part of the human digestive tract. Its main function is to store unabsorbed food waste and to absorb water and other body fluids before the waste is eliminated. Problems occur when polyps, which are small growths, appear in the lining of the colon. Polyps are not cancer, but if left where they are, they can develop into cancer. If untreated long enough, the cancer can not only block the colon but spread to other areas of the body. When that happens, it is usually fatal.

But a colonoscopy, which allows a doctor to look into the entire colon, can detect and remove most polyps and prevent cancers from forming. The procedure is done with an endoscopy, an instrument with a tiny video camera on the end of a flexible tube. The test usually takes less than an hour and requires day and night-before preparation and light sedation on the operating table.

If a colonoscopy will significantly reduce the deaths from colon cancer in the United States, why not just make sure that people get tested? The answer is money. A colonoscopy is expensive. The cost depends on insurance plans, where the patient lives, where the test is performed, and which doctor does it, but the typical costs range from $500 to $1,000.

Medicare covers a colonoscopy once every ten years for those fifty and older and at average risk. But for those below the age of fifty with some indication of bowel problems, the cost may be prohibitive even for those with some medical insurance plans. However, most insurance plans do cover a colonoscopy, at least partially. For those Americans without medical insurance, the $1,000 or higher cost may mean going without a test that could save lives.

Another area where money makes a difference in medical care is a trend that some patients' rights advocates find worrisome. It is the growth of what is called customized or concierge care or Doctor Boutiques, although most involved don't like the name.

A boutique doctor generally sees one hundred to five hundred patients a year. By contrast, other doctors probably see 2,000 to 3,000 patients during the same period. The boutique doctor may charge patients anywhere from $1,500 to $10,000 a year and, according to the American College of Physicians, fees can be as high as $20,000. For that fee, a patient can expect several perks. For example, someone who suffers an injury—a broken arm, for example—in an accident at home may call the boutique doctor at any hour and expect that he or she will appear in a reasonable time. The doctor will examine the injury and if a visit to the hospital is required, he or she will accompany the patient. Unless a hospital stay is required, the doctor will make sure the patient returns home safely.

A boutique doctor usually has well-furnished offices with comfortable sofas and chairs. Cake or fruit and coffee or tea are available while the patient waits. The wait is not very long.

For those who can afford these services, the cost is well worth it. It is very reassuring to know that your doctor is always available for you. In addition, the boutique doctor takes care of making any appointments for specialists or medical procedures. Besides getting a quick response in an emergency or having other medical needs handled personally, these patients can always be assured of getting a doctor's appointment on the day they call, or the following day at the very latest. According to a *New York Times* article,

> **One promise made to patients paying for concierge service is that waiting will not be a part of their health care experience. Patients are guaranteed that phone calls will be returned promptly, appointments will be scheduled on a same-day basis if necessary, and appointment times will be honored. A bowl of fruit salad and platters of bagels and sponge cake set out for patients in the waiting room can go barely touched over the course of a day, and the television often plays to an empty couch.**

It is truly luxury care.

For doctors who change to this new area, they say the rewards are equally great. For one thing, they have lots of time to spend with their patients. They claim this type of practice allows them to be better doctors. They also claim to save money for insurance companies because their patients rarely end up in emergency rooms. A patient with a boutique doctor may or may not be paid back by Medicare or other insurers. That means the patient must pay for house calls and possibly even for any hospital services in addition to the annual fee. Boutique doctors, meanwhile, typically earn three times as much a year as do other physicians.

The number of boutique doctors in the United States

is not large, but the trend is growing. Dr. Leslie Squires is unusual in that he runs both a boutique and a regular practice. He has two different waiting rooms, one of which is stylishly furnished. He admits that other doctors are skeptical, but, he says, "This is the way medicine has to go in San Francisco. . . . I'm sort of like home base. If I can't solve the problem myself, I know where to send people."

If boutique medicine is the trend, there are a number of detractors. Many lawmakers criticize a growing medical system that is based on excluding those without the money to pay for these services.

"Philosophically, I think it's appalling," says David Barton Smith, health services administration professor at Temple University, Philadelphia. "It's creating a two-class system of medicine."

Some critics fear that the growth of luxury care will leave fewer traditional doctors in the field to take care of all the other patients, thus compromising patients' rights. The average doctor today sees about 112 patients a week and spends 10.6 minutes with each one. The boutique doctor sees about thirty patients a week and spends thirty minutes with each. "I think it's scary and unprofessional to think the level of care is scaled to the fee," says Jay Jacobson of LDS Hospital and the University of Utah School of Medicine, Salt Lake City.

Other Limits to Choice

Another area that has the potential to discriminate against the poor regarding health and medical practices is the U.S. welfare system. Although its aim is aid to needy people and families, it places many limits on work and the ability to earn a salary.

In 1935, the welfare of poor children and other dependent people became a federal government responsi-

AS PEOPLE LIVE LONGER LIVES, MANY FIND THEMSELVES IN NURSING HOMES, AND MANY OF THOSE PEOPLE RELY ON GOVERNMENT-FUNDED MEDICARE TO PAY THEIR MEDICAL EXPENSES. HERE, ST. LOUIS, MO, NURSING HOME RESIDENT HAZEL EMERY LISTENS TO A DISCUSSION DURING A NEWS CONFERENCE CONCERNING $37 MILLION MISSOURI WAS SCHEDULED TO LOSE IN FEDERAL FUNDS FOR NURSING HOMES.

bility. During the Great Depression of the 1930s, an overwhelming number of Americans needed food, clothing, and shelter. The effect on children was especially severe. It was thought that as employment improved in the

United States, the need for federal aid would wither away. It did not.

The welfare system has greatly expanded since that time. New programs were added, such as President Lyndon Johnson's War on Poverty, which gave cash benefits to needy persons. In 1964, Congress provided a food-stamp program for low-income households. In 1974, the Supplemental Security Income (SSI) program was established to help the needy elderly, blind, and disabled. By 1994, the Aid to Families with Dependent Children (AFDC) supported more than 14 million children and their parents. As the welfare system grew, so did its critics.

Most of the criticism against the system is that it lets able-bodied adults avoid work and become dependent on the government. Most AFDC families, for instance, have the children in the home cared for by a mother who does not work outside the home.

President Bill Clinton tried to change the system in 1996. The Personal Responsibility and Work Opportunity Relocation Act turns authority over to the states to design welfare programs and get people to work. So far, Wisconsin has the strictest work requirements for those receiving aid. Only mothers with children under three months old are temporarily exempt from going to work. Issues of welfare reform still being debated in Congress and the states include: a limit in years on the benefits welfare families may receive; whether able-bodied people without minor children and without a job should be limited to no more than three months of food stamps in a five-year period; and if a person on welfare is assigned to community-service work, should he or she be paid at a rate equal to the minimum wage?

A patient's rights may also be limited by hospital rules. A seven-year research study, ending in 2001, looked at the length of time patients stayed in the hospital for rehabilitation. It investigated about 149,000 patients at some 744 rehab centers in 48 states. The average patient age was 68 years.

The study was started because in the mid–1990s, managed care facilities began to reduce their payments for rehab stays. In 2002, Medicare started a payment system that pays hospitals a fixed amount based on the patient's condition regardless of what the hospital actually charges. This has led to shorter stays for rehabilitation after such conditions as strokes, heart attacks, hip fractures, and other neurological disorders.

The study suggested that the practice of discharging such patients leaves them with a greater chance of earlier death. According to the study, the average stay in the hospital for those suffering from broken bones and other disabling conditions dropped 40 percent. The death rate at the same time rose nearly 4 percent. Shorter stays may not be the cause of increased mortality rates, but there seems to be a relationship.

Charging another infringement of patients' rights, deaf patients sued Laurel Regional Hospital in Prince George's County, Maryland, in January 2005. The hospital serves a large population near Gallaudet University, for deaf and hard of hearing students. According to the suit, hearing-impaired patients cannot understand their diagnoses and cannot get satisfactory answers to their questions because the hospital violates the rights of deaf people. Laurel does not, says the suit, have sign language interpreters available at medical consultations, nor does it provide adequate communication between patients and emergency room staff. As such, it is claimed that the hospital violates the Americans with Disabilities Act.

Specifically, the suit charges that six patients could not get medical attention because no one at the hospital could speak with them. No interpreters for the deaf were provided. In addition, one deaf patient in the suit charges mistreatment by a hospital worker. The patient was lying on a bed in the emergency room after a spinal tap, as she was told to do, when the worker, not knowing she was deaf and failing to communicate, dragged her off the bed. The woman continues to suffer problems from the experience.

A hospital spokesperson says that changes are occurring. At least one hospital in the area, Howard County General, has on-call interpreters who can get to the hospital within thirty minutes.

5

In the Hospital, Nursing Home, and Doctor's Office

Of the more than 5,000 hospitals in the United States, most are nonprofit, community institutions, or voluntary or general hospitals, including academic medical centers. They account for two-thirds of the approximately 37 million hospital admissions in the United States each year. Other hospitals are owned by local, state, or federal governments and for-profit, private institutions, which sometimes form a chain of hospitals and have one corporate owner. If a hospital is connected to a medical school and offers a teaching program, it is called a teaching hospital.

Any hospital is organized and run like a business organization because that's what it is. A nonprofit, community hospital generally has a board of directors, usually made up of local business leaders. But the real operation of the hospital is the charge of the chief administrator, who may be called the president or director. More often than not, the director comes from a business rather than medical background. Other employees cover all aspects of the twenty-four-hour-a-day business of a hospital such as admittance procedures, billing, and publicity.

When a person enters a hospital, he or she is under the care of his or her regular doctor, who is called the attending physician. But many other people are involved in the recovery process. In a teaching hospital, for instance, the medical staff is made up of interns and residents. Interns are doctors who have completed medical school and are now in training in a hospital setting. They are supervised by residents, who may be in their second or third year of hospital work. These medical personnel make daily rounds. They visit each patient and ask questions about treatment. In turn, the trainees are supervised by a chief

IN TERMS OF INTERACTION WITH PATIENTS, NURSES ARE KEY. A NATIONWIDE NURSING SHORTAGE LED TO A DEMONSTRATION—WITH EMPTY, USED NURSING SHOES IN THE FOREGROUND—AT THE U.S. CAPITOL BUILDING ON MAY 9, 2001. THE NURSES WERE CALLING FOR LEGISLATION TO ESTABLISH STAFFING STANDARDS, BAN MANDATORY OVERTIME, AND HELP SOLVE THE NURSING SHORTAGE.

resident and a staff doctor, who is in charge of the overall hospital training. A hospital also has consultants, doctors who specialize in some aspect of medicine and may be called upon to offer opinions on treatment.

But the hospital staff members whom patients see most often during a stay are the nurses. There are many types of nurses, depending on years and types of study. Some nurses have masters' degrees in nursing, some hold a bachelors of science degree, or one from a two-year nursing program. Some nurses graduated from a nursing school affiliated with a hospital. In addition, there are licensed practical nurses (LPNs) and aides. The LPN has completed a licensed practical nursing program and is qualified to work under the supervision of an RN.

The goal of all hospitals is to care for the sick. But all hospitals are not alike in terms of quality of care and expertise of the staff and administration. As author Melvin Urofsky noted in *Letting Go:*

> **In an ideal world, perhaps, the interests of patients, families, doctors, hospitals, and courts would all coincide. But aside from the fact that this is an imperfect world, the interests of these groups are not necessarily congruent.... Hospitals caught in a crunch between escalating expenses and new technology, must weigh costs that never before mattered. Moreover, in a society as litigious as ours [meaning very quick to sue in court], doctors and hospitals walk in constant fear that a "wrong" judgment will lead to a ruinous lawsuit.**

Who Watches the Hospitals?

Considering the life-and-death nature of their work, it may seem odd to learn that until 1946 very few states had any laws regulating hospitals. At that time, Congress passed

Who Checks On the Hospitals?

Not only doctors can be sued for poor or harmful practices. Health departments in each state are charged with policing state medical institutions. For example, in April 2006, the Health Department of New York State cited Northern Westchester Hospital in Mount Kisco for six deficiencies in its care of a sixty-eight-year-old woman. Among the most serious was the charge that the hospital treated her for hip pain instead of the two fractured hip bones she actually had. The day after she was discharged, the woman, who suffered other ailments as well, was admitted to another hospital where she died two days later.

the Hill-Burton Hospital Survey and Construction Act. This was in response to President Harry Truman's proposal to improve the physical buildings of the nation's hospital system. Suddenly, most states adopted licensing hospital laws. But that was mainly because the act said that Congress would not release funds for hospital construction unless there was such a law in place.

Another change occurred in 1951. The American College of Physicians, the American Hospital Association, the American Medical Association, and the Canadian Medical Association (which later left to form its own group) joined with the American College of Surgeons, founded in 1913. They formed the Joint Commission on Accreditation of Hospitals, which began to publish hospital standards in 1953. The American Association of Homes for the Aging and the American Nursing Home Association joined the group in 1987. The name was changed to the present Joint Commission on Accreditation of Healthcare Organizations (JCAHO).

The hospital or other outpatient facility volunteers for accreditation, which means that it okays a comprehensive evaluation of its services and operations. The governing board of JCAHO includes doctors and nurses, medical directors, and consumers. JCAHO doctors and nurses personally visit the facility to be accredited. They conduct a review that looks at the safety of the environment provided for patients, whether patients' rights are being protected, and whether the facility educates its patients about the options and risks of treatment in the facility.

Since its beginning, the JCAHO has expanded its area of activities, including accreditation for home care and managed care organizations. In 2006, reflecting modern medical breakthroughs, it announced a certification program for organ transplant centers.

Even with changes to assure patients' rights and good

care, there remain problems with hospital standards. In early 2006, congressional leaders voiced concerns that many nonprofit hospitals do not provide enough charity work, or at least minimum care to the poor, to justify their tax-exempt status. Legislators said that if the medical industry doesn't set higher standards, they will have to.

The basic standards for granting tax exemptions to hospitals have changed very little in the United States since 1969. Before then, a hospital had to provide charity care or lose its tax-exempt status. But since that time, critics say the Internal Revenue Service (IRS) has not been so demanding when it studies hospital exemptions. There has been an increase in lawsuits against hospitals by low-income people, who claim they receive few free or reduced-price services.

Some states have taken action over these concerns. After former patients in Kansas complained that some nonprofit hospitals hired debt collection agencies to harass them, the attorney general promised an investigation. In Illinois, new legislation was introduced to make hospitals provide at least minimum charity care, about 8 percent of operating costs. The attorney general of Minnesota also proposed stronger laws in early 2006. He said that some nonprofit hospitals in the state give their top executives excessive gifts but don't give even minimum charity care to those who need it.

Privacy

Can anyone really expect privacy in a hospital setting? "The old 'rule' in the hospital was that 'everyone has access to the patient's medical record except the patient'; the modern rule is that everyone (including the patient) has access." Obviously, information in a hospital has to be shared if a patient is to be treated. The concern has always been: shared with whom and how much information? For instance, all cases of child abuse must be reported. So must contagious diseases, injuries such as gunshot wounds, or death under suspicious circumstances.

In 1996, Congress enacted the Health Insurance Portability and Accountability Act (HIPAA). It protects health insurance coverage for workers and their families when they change or lose their jobs. It also requires the establishment of national standards for electronic health care transactions.

The Privacy Rule took effect in April 2003. It regulates the use and disclosure of Protected Health Information (PHI). That includes any data about health status, provision of health care, or payment for health care. It covers any part of a patient's medical record and payment history. In so doing, it requires the patient to sign a goodly number

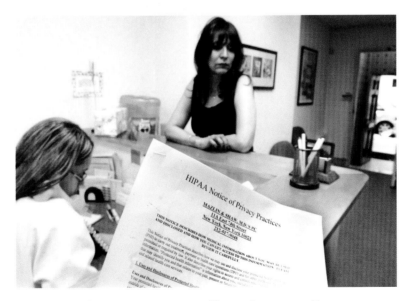

IN 1996, CONGRESS ENACTED THE HEALTH INSURANCE PORTABILITY AND ACCOUNTABILITY ACT, WHICH ESTABLISHES SEVERAL RIGHTS FOR PATIENTS, INCLUDING MANDATING THAT PATIENT RECORDS REMAIN PRIVATE.

of forms. The standards limit ways in which hospitals and other health-care facilities can use medical information, whether the records are on paper, in computers, or transmitted orally. Institutions that violate the law face financial penalties or prison terms.

When can medical personnel discuss medical information about a patient? For example, a woman may go to the emergency room complaining of chest pains. The tests for a heart attack are negative. However, she tells the ER doctor that she had a similar attack a few years earlier when living in another city. The ER doctor can legitimately call the other doctor to discuss the woman's condition.

But what if the ER doctor decides to discuss his patient's chest pains with a golfing partner, who also happens to be a doctor? That is okay too, *provided* the ER doctor does not use the patient's name or talk about her in such a way that she can be identified.

What if the woman's doctor calls the ER doctor? If the patient gives her consent, the doctor can give out the information. If she does not give consent, the doctor can only say such things as "stable" or "no change."

Medical Records

Every year, about a billion visits are made to U.S. health-care facilities. And each time a visit is made—to a doctor's office, a hospital, a clinic, or any other health-care site—another medical record is created or added to. Much of the data is necessary and proper to provide for continuing care and to keep financial records straight. The JCAHO says that proper medical records should contain: medical history of the patient, outcome of physical exam, what the diagnosis was, informed consent sheet or explanation of why there isn't one, and any test and procedure reports.

What about a patient's privacy concerning medical records? The HHS has this to say:

Patients generally should be able to see and obtain copies of their medical records and request corrections if they identify errors and mistakes. Health plans, doctors, hospitals, clinics, nursing homes and other covered entities generally should provide access to these records within 30 days and may charge patients for the cost of copying and sending the records.

In general, patients have a right to see their medical records. But why would you want to? Would you even understand your records without the help of a doctor? The answers differ, of course. You might want to see your own medical record just so you can understand your condition and treatment more fully. You might be moving across the country and want to carry a record of your past treatment with you. As for reading and understanding your records, you should be able to get by with the help of a good medical dictionary—that is, of course, if you can read the doctor's handwriting!

Extended care facilities in the United States are also concerned with privacy of information and medical records. For the past several years, there has been a growing trend for those sixty-five and older to move into retirement communities. An example is Kendal on Hudson, a Continuing Care Retirement Community overlooking the Hudson River in Westchester County, New York. It offers independent living, assisted living, and skilled nursing care on the same site. A director of health services, medical director, and team of licensed nurses oversee the health care of Kendal residents. Those sixty-five and older enter into a contract when they choose Kendal or other such health-care facilities. The contract entitles them to the use of their apartment for their lifetime as well as lifetime health care.

People who are sixty-five or older in good health may, for instance, move into an independent living apartment at Kendal that looks like any well-appointed, well-laid-out apartment anywhere. However, there are differences. The bathrooms at Kendal are large enough for a wheelchair and are equipped with grab bars for safety. There is an emergency call system in the bedrooms and bathrooms. The resident simply pulls the cord to receive immediate medical attention. In addition, residents are given an emergency pendant to wear around their necks in case they need help quickly.

If a Kendal resident becomes ill and needs temporary assistance or rehabilitation following surgery, he or she may be moved within Kendal to one of twenty-four enriched housing units. Besides receiving housing and meals, the resident is assisted with daily living activities such as bathing or dressing. The resident stays in this unit until fully recovered, at which time he or she returns to the independent apartment.

If a person requires more medical help, he or she may move temporarily or permanently into the forty-two-bed skilled nursing center fully licensed by New York State. There, twenty-four-hour nursing care is provided. This style of living is expensive because it provides health-care practices for people who can afford it.

Kendal, like many such facilities, issues a document to all residents concerning privacy information. It states, among other things, that Kendal is committed to preserving the rights of its residents about all medical practices and records. It will only disclose health information with the permission of the resident. The disclosure is done in three ways: treatment, payment, and health-care operations. Treatment involves giving information to any doctors and other medical personnel who are involved in a person's health care. Payment means that the records will be used in dealing with insurance companies as well as

Medical Report Cards

The U.S. government's Centers for Medicare and Medicaid Services has decided that citizens should be better informed about the treatment they get from doctors and hospitals. Launched in April 2005, its Web site—hospitalcompare.hhs.gov—lets people look at the records of more than 4,000 hospitals across the country. Users can study records of three conditions: pneumonia, heart attack, and heart failure, a condition in which the heart muscle weakens and cannot pump blood efficiently. No death rates are given. Some advocacy groups hope that this is one small step toward improving the quality of U.S. health care.

Kendal's own billing system. Health-care operations include those in Kendal itself, such as the staff, who might need to know about medical conditions of the residents in order serve them.

Elder Care: Rights in Nursing Homes

When a person needs care outside the home, the first question should be: what kind? There are a number of different places for outside care depending on individual needs. Group homes might work for someone who needs housekeeping services more than direct medical care. People, usually the elderly, live together in a house that is supervised by a twenty-four-hour-a-day staff that can provide basic necessities such as help with bathing or taking blood pressure. Most of these homes cannot handle people with serious medical conditions.

Assisted living facilities offer private or semiprivate rooms with communal dining and living areas. Staff can help with basic medical needs but not skilled nursing care. This type of facility is usually located near a nursing center or other health facility.

The skilled care site is for those with major medical needs, and it offers extensive nursing services depending on the condition of the patient. The patient must be admitted by a doctor, and expenses are covered to greater or lesser degree by Medicare, Medicaid, or other types of insurance. There are two basic types of skilled care facilities: rehabilitation and special. A patient admitted for rehab care usually is recovering from major surgery or serious injury, such as a broken back. The patient needs major medical care at the time but is expected to return home able to care for himself or herself within a short period. Medicare usually covers these costs. Special care facilities may tend to those who need feeding tubes or ventilators, for example. Some special care units deal with people suffering from mental problems such as dementia. These conditions may cause a person to act aggressively or become disoriented. Special care facilities have specially trained staff to deal with such problems.

For those people in the last stages of cancer or other fatal disease, there is also hospice care. The care focuses on compassion and making the patient as comfortable as possible. The volunteers, either in special hospital homes or in the individual's home, provide support to both the patient and family.

Long-term care, which the term *nursing home* brings to mind, usually implies that the patient will no longer be able to live independently. That would generally be the case, for instance, with someone suffering from Alzheimer's. It also implies that the medical care is aimed more at keeping the patient safe and well-maintained than at restoring health. Medicare does not generally cover the cost of long-term care. Expenses are normally covered by long-term-care insurance and, for those who qualify, by Medicaid.

The staff of a well-run nursing home consists of many people in different capacities. It is headed by a director, who manages the day-to-day operation. The medical director is a doctor in charge of medical policies. In addition, each patient in the nursing home has an attending physician who oversees the person's medical needs. The all-important nursing staff usually consists of a director of nursing, an RN in charge of overall care; a charge nurse who heads each working shift; and the line staff, RNs who do the nursing work such as taking blood. LPNs and nursing aides are also part of the nursing team. In addition, the nursing home generally has a social services director who watches over such needs as a patient's adjustment to the facility; a dietary services director in charge of nutrition; and an activities director who plans social events for the residents. Some nursing homes also have clergy on staff; others bring in outside clergy for services.

Nursing homes often get a bad rap, although most are good and competent. But as do hospital patients, nursing home patients have legal rights. They are ensured by state and federal law. These are some of the rights ensured to nursing home patients:

• **Privacy. Staff cannot give out information about a patient without his or permission.**

• **Protection. Nursing home residents have the right not to be sexually, physically, or emotionally abused.**

• **Finances. A resident, if competent, has the legal right to manage his or her money or to designate someone to do so.**

• **Dignity. All nursing home patients have the legal right to receive respect in treatment.**

In addition to the residents, family members also have rights in the nursing home. They have the right to be told of any changes in the care of their loved ones. They also have the right to question how their loved ones are being treated, both physically and emotionally. But as with rights in hospitals and other health-care facilities, patients' rights supersede those of the family. A competent nursing home patient may withhold information from family members if he or she so chooses.

Rights of People with Privacy Concerns about Illness

There are many reasons why a person might wish to keep his or her illness secret or private. An example is someone infected with the Human Immunodeficiency Virus, or HIV.

According to the U.S. Centers for Disease Control and Prevention, more than 850,000 people in the United States are infected with HIV. It is a worldwide epidemic. Acquired Immune Deficiency Syndrome (AIDS) refers to life-threatening medical conditions that develop as a result of infection with the Human Immunodeficiency Virus (HIV). HIV destroys the human immune system, which protects people from disease.

Although the virus that causes these illnesses has been identified since 1981, we still know very little about how it destroys the immune system or how to stop it. However, new drug treatments now allow people with HIV to live longer, healthier lives. As a result, many with HIV can hold regular jobs for longer periods. That brings up the question of legal rights and privacy in the workplace concerning those who are HIV-positive.

A person who is HIV-positive is considered disabled according to the Americans with Disabilities Act (ADA), passed by the U.S. Congress in 1990. That act governs the rights of all people with disabilities and applies to workplaces employing fifteen or more people. It also prohibits employer discrimination in all work-related activities. These nondiscrimination laws also apply to health-care providers, such as doctors' and dentists' offices, clinics, hospitals, government nursing homes and hospices, and substance abuse treatment centers.

Those with HIV are also protected in the workplace in three specific areas: confidentiality, discrimination, and medical leave.

Confidentiality: A person with HIV does not have to give out such information when applying for a job, and a prospective employer can't ask for it. The employer can ask only if the applicant is "fit" to do

the job. However, a medical exam may be called for after a job offer has been made and if it is necessary for job performance. Any data on HIV status must be kept in a confidential medical file and brought out only on a "need to know" basis.

Discrimination: A person with HIV can be fired from a job for the same reasons that non-HIV workers would be fired, such as lateness or poor performance. But a person cannot be fired because of his or her medical condition.

Accommodation: If a worker is HIV-positive, the employer has to make what are called "reasonable" accommodations for the workers at the job site. The term "reasonable" applies to both worker and employer. The accommodation might be as simple as letting the worker have time off for medical examinations.

Those with HIV are also protected under the Family and Medical leave Act (FMLA). It protects workers' jobs if they must take time off to care for a sick spouse, parent, child, or themselves.

In addition, medical personnel cannot refuse to treat those who are HIV-positive *unless* they can show that by treating them, the safety of others would be in jeopardy. This is difficult to prove, however. A doctor may refer an HIV-infected person to another health-care provider, but only if professional judgment would seem to promise better care.

Do Patients Have Courtesy Rights?

Suppose a friend has a serious back problem that could make him permanently disabled if it is not treated. But the specialist recommended by his own doctor is rude and arrogant. Is the friend stuck with a rude, arrogant doctor just because the specialist's knowledge is needed?

Not necessarily, says Dr. Richard Frankel, professor of medicine and geriatrics at Indiana University. The idea is to be prepared *before* the office visit. According to Frankel, patients have on average "18 seconds to talk to a doctor before they are interrupted . . . women doctors interrupt at the same rate as men. The trick for patients is to decide ahead of time what they want to convey and to deflect interruptions to say it."

Frankel advises the patient to make a list of complaints and ask the doctor to staple it to his or her chart. After the office visit, the patient should write or send an e-mail message to the doctor talking about the experience. A copy of the letter sent to the medical director of the doctor's practice often also gets results, he says.

One of the most common complaints about the U.S. medical profession is about how much time is spent waiting in a doctor's office. Your appointment is for 9:30 a.m. and you're still sitting there at 11:45 a.m. There are, of course, legitimate reasons for delays in doctors' offices and other medical settings. Emergencies can foul up appointments for the day. More typically, doctors overschedule in an effort not to have a free moment during office hours or an empty waiting room. Some chalk that up to greed or a lack of sympathy for what the patient goes through. Some doctors claim that insurance companies reimburse them at lower rates than in the past. Therefore, there is more pressure to see more patients.

According to researchers in the health-care field, the waiting problem for patients has only gotten worse. With medical advances, more patients must go through more tests and procedures. Patients now take more medicines and undergo more treatments, which all means more visits to a doctor's office.

Coming Trend in Patient Care?

An often-heard complaint in a doctor's office or a local emergency room is the long waiting time. Now, perhaps relief may be coming from an unlikely source—the nation's biggest retailers. Companies such as CVS, Wal-Mart, Rite Aid, and Target are giving space to walk-in clinics with names such as Minute-Clinic or RediClinic. They offer quick treatment for such ailments as sore throat, flu, and infections.

These walk-in clinics are staffed by licensed nurse practitioners who can write prescriptions. They also send the patient on to a doctor if that is warranted. And most accept health insurance or Medicare. The average cost is estimated at between $45 and $60, better than the average doctor's visit, which runs about $74. The waiting time is generally cut in half. And in the unlikely event that you have to wait for a while in a walk-in clinic, the retailers hope you'll spend the time shopping in the store.

AARP, July & August, 2006

No matter what the reason, there is—unfortunately for the patient—no law that gives you courtesy rights or protects you from a long, boring, and often anxious wait. If you are spending too much time in a doctor's office, you might have to grin and bear it or possibly call ahead to find out how long the wait will be . . . or find another doctor.

6

The Abortion Debate and Stem Cell Research

Two Supreme Court decisions in the twentieth century were especially important in defining rights and limits in the areas of contraception and abortion. *Griswold* v. *Connecticut* (1965) is a little-known but important case. An 1879 law in Connecticut made it illegal to anyone to use any drug, article, or instrument to prevent conception. A suit was started by two members of the Planned Parenthood League of Connecticut who had been charged with violating the law because they gave information to married couples on preventing conception. The highest court in Connecticut agreed with the charge. But by a vote of 7 to 2, the Supreme Court reversed the decision. It said, among other things, that the law was invalid because it infringed on the privacy rights of married persons.

In 1973, the High Court issued one of its most controversial decisions. It decided in *Roe* v. *Wade* that most laws against abortion violate a woman's constitutional right to privacy. Abortion is defined as the termination of a pregnancy before the embryo has developed and could survive outside the uterus. The Court decision inflamed a growing national debate between pro-choice and anti-abortion camps. It is in many ways tied to a newer controversy: the rights of those involved in—and those who stand to benefit from—stem cell research.

Abortion, The Law

In March 1970, lawyers for Jane Roe (an alias for Norma McCorvey) filed a suit in a Texas court against the state law that made abortion a crime except for "medical advice for the purpose of saving the life of the mother." The suit claimed that the Texas laws violated rights guaranteed to pregnant women by the First, Fourth, Fifth, Ninth, and Fourteenth Amendments to the Constitution. In Dallas County, Texas, district attorney Henry Wade was the defendant in the case. A three-judge district court decided for Roe, but it did not stop enforcement of the laws.

The case was appealed to the U.S. Supreme Court, headed by Chief Justice Warren Burger, and argued on December 13, 1971. The decision, voiced by Justice Harry Blackmun, cited the Texas law as too vague. But Burger pushed for reargument and the other justices agreed. Supposedly they were not impressed with the initial oral presentation of the case. However, Justice William O. Douglas was apparently angry over the decision to reargue. He thought that Burger, a close friend of President Richard Nixon, wanted the decision put off until after the November 1972 elections.

Nonetheless, the case was reargued and the decision announced on January 22, 1973. By a 7 to 2 majority, the Supreme Court struck down the Texas abortion laws. Only Justices Byron White and William Rehnquist were opposed. The decision found that the laws "violated the woman's right to privacy, which the opinion located in the due process clause of the Fourteenth Amendment."

SINCE *ROE* V. *WADE* WAS DECIDED BY THE SUPREME COURT IN
1973, WOMEN HAVE HAD THE RIGHT TO MAKE DECISIONS ON
WHETHER TO TERMINATE THEIR PREGNANCIES BEFORE TERM. IT
ALL STARTED WITH NORMA MCCORVEY (LEFT), THEN KNOWN,
ANONYMOUSLY, AS JANE ROE. HERE SHE IS PICTURED WALKING
WITH HER ATTORNEY, GLORIA ALLRED, TO HEAR THE CASE.

The right to privacy, said the Court, was broad enough to cover a woman's decision to end her pregnancy. The Court also set limits, such as that the privacy right does not extend into the third trimester, or last three months, of pregnancy.

There was immediate controversy over the ruling, and it continues today. Those who applaud the decision say it preserves a woman's equality and personal freedom and that it signifies individual rights over collective rights. Those who oppose it argue that the fetus is a human life. They say that life begins at conception; therefore, the unborn are alive and must be legally protected. Such support comes mainly from the Catholic Church and other religious organizations and conservative groups.

Since the 1973 decision, there have been many attempts to whittle away at *Roe* v. *Wade* or overturn it completely. A nominee's stand on the abortion law continues to figure prominently in Supreme Court hearings. It is generally the major concern—and often develops into a royal battle—whenever a president has the opportunity to nominate someone for the nation's highest court. Such was the case when Ronald Reagan picked Robert Bork in 1987. Ultraconservatives pressured Reagan to name Bork, who was at the time a District of Columbia federal appeals judge. Reagan did so, and it brought about one of the major political battles of his second term.

The decision was crucial to both liberals and conservatives because at the time the Court was evenly divided. Four justices were generally considered to be on the moderate voting side and four were conservative. With the retirement of Lewis Powell, Reagan, a conservative himself, had the chance to swing the Court. But Bork's views on abortion and *Roe* v. *Wade* became the focal point in his testimony before the Judiciary Committee. Politicians voiced their views in newspapers and on television.

After five days of testimony, Bork was turned down by a vote of 9 to 5. Anthony Kennedy, a conservative who had a broad view of constitutional rights, was then nominated and appointed.

The views on abortion and *Roe* v. *Wade* of prospective candidates for the Court as well as for the presidency and Congress are still of major concern. John Kerry's pro-choice stand when he ran against George W. Bush for the presidency in 2004 reportedly cost him many votes. The most recent Supreme Court members, Chief Justice John Roberts appointed in late 2005 and Samuel Alito (early 2006), were grilled sharply about their views before they were eventually confirmed.

Some have tried to pass laws aimed at overturning *Roe* v. *Wade*. On March 6, 2006, the South Dakota legislature made most abortions punishable as a crime, even in the case of pregnancies caused by rape or incest. It was the first state legislature to pass a law that openly challenged *Roe* v. *Wade*. Some people hoped the South Dakota ban would find its way to the Supreme Court so that *Roe* could be overturned. However, on November 7, 2006, South Dakota voters repealed the ban by a margin of 55 to 49 percent.

Besides the law that protects a woman's right to have an abortion if she so decides, other rights concerning pregnancy and birth are also protected. For instance, a married woman who is competent does not have to get the consent of her husband for any type of treatment, including pregnancy care or sterilization.

Other rights concerning pregnancy and birth include: a patient being examined by a male doctor has the right to have another woman in the examining room with her. This generally applies only to women because obstetrics and gynecology specialists are overwhelmingly male. (This right protects not only the woman from possible improper advances by the doctor but it protects the doctor from false charges against him.) A woman has the right to refuse a caesarean operation, although in some cases the doctor or hospital may refuse to perform it. She also has the right to refuse a caesarean even if she is dying and the fetus is still alive. A woman has the right to give birth at home. Qualifications for other home birth attendants such as nurse midwives vary from state to state.

In 2000, Doris Haire of the American Foundation for Maternal and Child Health drew up the Pregnant Patient's Bill of Rights. It acknowledges the doctor's legal obligation to get informed consent from a pregnant patient. As stated in the *Standards for Obstetric-Gynecologic Services* of the American College of Obstetricians and Gynecologists (ACOG):

It is important to note the distinction between "consent" and "informed consent." Many physicians, because they do not realize there is a difference, believe they are free from liability if the patient consents to treatment. This is not true. The physician may still be liable if the patient's consent was not informed. In addition, the usual consent obtained by a hospital does not in any way release the physician from his legal duty of obtaining an informed consent from his patient.

What makes consent *informed*? The doctor must explain the medical process to be performed and whether it is new or unusual. Risks of treatment must be outlined as well as chances of recovery. Why the treatment is necessary and whether there may be alternative treatments must also be explained.

The Pregnant Patient's Bill of Rights, issued by the American Hospital Association, lists sixteen specific rights. Few women know of this statement, and it is not routinely presented in all hospitals. Besides the rights of informed consent, other rights include the right to be told the brand and generic drug names of any medication; the right to know the name of the person who will administer a drug during labor or birth; the right to have someone close to her during labor and birth; the right to know the name and qualifications of the person who actually delivers the baby; and the right to complete access to her hospital medical records.

Stem Cell Research

Another issue with the potential for explosion is stem cell research. For some, it once again brings up the question of the value of human life at its beginning. For others, it is a matter of who has a right to the embryos involved and who—if anyone—has the right to rein in science. An article by Father Mark Hodges in 2006 stated: "A raging debate is going on in our nation now, over whether or not taxes should support killing human embryos in order to harvest their stem cells for experimentation."

Stem cells are different from all other cells in the human body. They are different for three important reasons. (1) Stem cells can divide and renew themselves for long periods. Muscle cells, nerve cells, or blood cells, for instance, cannot. (2) Stem cells are unspecialized. That means they do not have any structures that allow them to perform specialized functions, in the way, for example, that a heart muscle cell pumps blood through the body. The heart muscle cell cannot be made to do the work of the nerve cell, for instance. (3) The unspecialized stem cells, under certain experimental conditions, can be made into cells with specialized functions. In other words, the stem cell can be made to do the work of the heart muscle cell. Scientists believe that stem cells can be made to do many kinds of work, such as producing insulin in the pancreas as a treatment or cure for diabetes. They may be made to produce dopamine neurons, which may eliminate the tremors of Parkinson's disease. Scientists see the potential of stem cells to treat spinal cord injury, arthritis, Alzheimer's, stroke, and all manner of heart problems. However, experimentation with this area of medical research is still young, and many questions remain unanswered.

The debate is not about the potential of stem cell research to alleviate suffering or cure illness, although some do question the scientific claims. The debate rages mainly over the use of embryonic stem cells, or as some see it, whether the embryo has rights to be protected.

Embryonic stem cells are taken from embryos, which are organisms in the earlier stage of development. In humans, this is generally described as the first three months after conception. These embryos develop from eggs donated for research and fertilized in the laboratory. They are not eggs fertilized in a woman's body. Typically, the embryonic stem cells are taken from embryos that are four to five days old.

Many religious and conservative groups base their objections to stem cell research on the destruction of these embryonic stem cells. They believe the embryos are the beginning of human life. Does that mean human life is destroyed by this research? Must the rights of the embryo be protected? Some groups think that the problem might be bypassed by using adult instead of embryonic stem cells. Adult stem cells are also found throughout the human body. They also divide and renew themselves. The problem is that at this stage of research, adult stem cells are limited in how many different cell types they can become. Embryonic stem cells can become all cell types of the body.

Many countries are faced with the dilemma over stem

cell research. The fight often pits the rights of the embryo against the rights of those who are suffering from diseases that could possibly be helped or cured by these medical advancements. The Netherlands, for example, passed the Embryo Act in September 2002. It sets conditions and restrictions on the use of embryos in that country.

The act bans production of embryos purely for research. However, people who have had in vitro fertilization (IVF) treatment may donate any unused embryos to a third party to produce embryonic stem cells for research. (*In vitro* is Latin for "in glass," which refers to test tubes even though neither test tubes nor glass is used. Even so, babies born from this procedure have been known as test tube babies.)

Those who undergo IVF treatment are generally couples who, for one reason or another, are unable to conceive naturally. The IVF treatment involves egg cells that have been removed from the woman's uterus. They are fertilized by sperm and transferred to the woman's uterus. Many eggs are fertilized in the hope that one will lead to pregnancy.

The scientific research in the Netherlands must be conducted under certain specified conditions. The research must be aimed at results that are medically important. All research programs must be approved by the Central Committee on Research involving Human Subjects (CCMO).

The United States has no embryo act, but the subject was raised heatedly in the presidential debates between George W. Bush and John Kerry in 2004. Occupying a ringside seat at one debate was Kerry supporter and television star Michael J. Fox, who suffers from Parkinson's disease, diagnosed in 1991.

In 2001, the Bush administration, which has been against most stem cell research, limited federal funds to the embryonic stem cell lines that were already created. At first this seemed like a compromise, with about seventy-eight stem cell lines, according to the government, available to scientists. But that figure soon dropped, according to the National Institutes of Health, to about twenty-three.

The government limits federal money to create new embryonic lines, but scientists may use private money for that purpose, and they do. Research university centers around the country report an increase in producing new stem cell lines. Some states passed laws on the subject of stem cell research. In California, for instance, in 2004, Proposition 71 stated: "Should the California Institute for Regenerative Medicine be established to regulate and fund stem cell research with the constitutional right to conduct such research and with an oversight committee? Prohibits funding of human reproductive cloning research." It was passed by California voters, 59.1 percent to 40.9 percent.

In February 2005, the House of Representatives passed the Stem Cell Research Enhancement Act to open up funding limited by the Bush Administration. The bill is still pending in the Senate.

In the meantime, work in this area continues around the world. In a *New York Times* report on May 20, 2005, a researcher in South Korea announced that he had produced human embryos through cloning and then extracting the stem cells. Researchers believed that Hwang Woo-Suk at Seoul National University had come upon a new method that might eliminate controversy over stem cell research. However, the claim proved fraudulent when it was found that Woo-Suk fabricated his research.

In a cloning process, the stem cells that come from the embryos are clones of the individuals. That means they are exact genetic matches. Which means if they were one day used to create plantable organs, pancreatic, insulin, or dopamine neurons, they would be less likely to be rejected by the patient's immune system, which is always a concern.

There is also interest in hematopoietic stem cells taken

from bone marrow. This method is used for people with blood or bone marrow diseases or certain types of cancer. Bone marrow cells that are infused intravenously could produce new blood cells. Still a risky procedure, it may help leukemia and other patients.

Although scientists around the world feel that the future looks promising for stem cell research, there have as yet been no cures with this technique. The fight over, in this case, the rights of the embryo—or when does human life begin?—continues. How far the opposing sides are from each other is perhaps best summed up in their remarks. Mary Tyler Moore, a diabetes victim, a pro-life Republican, and international chair of the Juvenile Diabetes Research Foundation, thinks that using leftover embryos for research is the same as organ donation. However, many religious groups feel that there is never a justification for tampering with embryos. "Cloning advocates have devoted themselves to a utilitarian ethic: The end justifies the means," says Richard M. Doerflinger, Deputy Director of the Secretariat for Pro-Life Activities, U.S. Conference of Catholic Bishops.

Moral concerns about the sanctity of human life, and the indignity of creating new lives in the lab simply to destroy them, were brushed aside. . . . By demeaning life, we learn to demean truth, rendering science itself meaningless. Whether scientists and lawmakers will learn this important lesson remains to be seen.

Yet, even with the Catholic Church, as well as in other religions, there is disagreement. Frank Cocozzelli, cofounder of the Committee for the Advancement of Stem Cell Research, is a Catholic who suffers from muscular dystrophy. He says "embryos that would otherwise be dis-

President George W. Bush Vetoes Stem Cell Bill

In June 2006, the U.S. Senate agreed to vote on a bill package intended to loosen restrictions on human embryonic stem cell research. It provided federal funding for research on embryos that were to be destroyed in fertility clinics. Scientists believe these embryos may be the key to cures for such diseases as diabetes and Parkinson's. On September 25, 2006, the president used his veto power for the first time to kill the bill. He said it was a moral issue.

MARY TYLER MOORE, WHO SUFFERS FROM LIFELONG DIABETES AND IS INTERNATIONAL CHAIR OF THE JUVENILE DIABETES RESEARCH FOUNDATION, IS A STRONG AND VOCAL SUPPORTER OF STEM-CELL RESEARCH.

carded should be salvaged for life: 'There's no dignity in watching people die unnecessarily.'"

The debate over rights to embryonic stem cells is likely to continue well into the future. Its outcome may depend upon medical advances in this area and whether the implied wonders of such research actually come true.

7

The Rights of Parents and Their Children

In June 2005, a bitter fight erupted between medical personnel in Texas and the parents of twelve-year-old Katie Wernecke. She suffered from Hodgkin's disease, a type of cancer that affects white blood cells and is part of the immune system. Doctors recommended radiation treatment. Katie's parents refused because they said the disease was in remission. At that point, Katie's mother took her daughter to a relative's farm in an attempt to hide her, but they were picked up by county police. The parents were relieved of custody.

According to the *New York Times*,

> The agreement on treatment appeared to douse another hot spot in the field of patients' rights. Coming on the heels of the polarizing right-to-die case of Terri Schiavo, Katie's case raised the provocative question of when parents lose their rights to control a child's medical treatment. Un-

der Texas law, parents may withhold medical treatment from a terminally ill child, but not in lesser situations.

Dr. Robert Klitzman, co-director of the Center for Bioethics at Columbia University in New York City, feels that the state has the right to interfere in a parent's decision when it is obvious that harm will result from withholding treatment. "Allowing a disease to inflict harm," he said, "is a form of child abuse."

However, a week after the Werneckes lost custody of Katie, new test results showed that the disease, which had apparently been in remission, was active once more. At that point, the Werneckes dropped their objection to radiation treatment. That ended what was shaping up as a duel over the rights of parents to make decisions for their minor children. Katie's parents explained that they had not opposed radiation for religious reasons. They wanted only to consult with other doctors on treatment.

Another battle for rights over child treatment caused a furor in London in 2004. Charlotte Wyatt was born prematurely at twenty-six weeks; the normal gestation period is thirty-six weeks. At age eleven months, she was still in the hospital where she was born. Sustained by a feeding tube and oxygen supply, she suffered severe brain damage as well as chronic heart and respiratory problems.

Doctors at the hospital believed that the infant felt nothing but constant pain. They asked the parents to allow them to remove the tubes that kept her alive. The patients refused on religious grounds. But in October, the courts agreed with the doctors. The judge said that it was not in the child's best interests to be kept alive under such conditions.

This fueled a fierce debate over who has the right to decide a child's medical treatment. The parents appealed the court's decision and won. At last reports, Charlotte is still alive and at home.

Who Has the Right?

In general, parents or legal guardians of minors (those under eighteen years of age) have the right to make decisions concerning a child's medical needs. But, as the cases of Katie Wernecke and Charlotte Wyatt illustrate, problems can occur when conflicts develop over serious illness and its treatment. There are exceptions to the rule that parents or guardians must give consent. Under certain conditions, even minors themselves have the right to decide on their own treatment.

CHARLOTTE WYATT WAS BORN PREMATURELY IN LONDON, ENGLAND, IN 2004, WITH SO MUCH DAMAGE TO HER SYSTEM THAT SHE WAS STILL IN THE HOSPITAL ELEVEN MONTHS LATER. HER MOTHER, DEBBIE WYATT, WANTED TO KEEP HER ALIVE BUT SHE LOST THE FIGHT TO THE DOCTORS WHO ARGUED THAT THE BABY FELT NOTHING BUT PAIN.

The conditions under which a minor can give consent to treatment vary somewhat from state to state. In general, most resemble the following examples taken from the state of California statutes.

Minors can give consent because of status: (1) they are married or divorced, (2) they are serving on active duty with the U.S. armed forces, (3) they are living away from home and taking care of themselves financially, or (4) they have been emancipated. Emancipation is a legal process by which a minor can under certain circumstances be given the same status as an adult to sign wills or consent to medical treatment. Not every state allows this option; California does under certain circumstances.

In California, certain statutes cover medical treatment for which a minor can give consent:

Rape. The minor must be twelve years or older to consent to treatment.

Sexual assault. The minor can be any age, but the doctor must try to inform the parents or guardian, unless the doctor believes they are the ones responsible for the assault.

Pregnancy and abortion. This right includes genetic counseling and any testing services that would be offered to a pregnant woman of any age.

Contagious and sexually transmitted diseases. In these cases, the minor must be twelve years or older to consent to treatment.

Drug or alcohol abuse. The minor must be twelve years or older, and the doctor must contact the parents or guardian. For this treatment, parents

in California have the right to ask for this care over the objection of the minor.

Mental health. On an outpatient basis for a minor twelve years or older or residential shelter services.

HIV tests. For minors twelve years or older.

According to U.S. law, all women, even those under the age of eighteen, are entitled to a safe, legal abortion as guaranteed by *Roe* v. *Wade*. However, many pregnant minors feel threatened because their own consent is not enough. In some states, although abortion is legal and parents consent is not required, they have to be notified.

The United States has the highest rate of teenage pregnancies in the world. Of the approximately 750,000 teenage pregnancies each year, almost all occur to unwed mothers and about 20 percent of those elect to have an abortion. Although most pregnant teens do tell at least one parent, many cannot because of broken homes or being victims of abuse, including sexual molestation.

Thirty-one states place limitations on a minor's right to abortion. Some laws are lenient or unenforced, but in eleven states at least one parent must give consent, or the doctor must get consent from the parent. Failure to do so can result in a loss of license by the health-care provider.

Sometimes, minors can give their consent for different types of medical treatment under certain unusual conditions. The parent or guardian may sign a form giving the minor consent if the child is going to be away at camp, for instance. In an emergency, a minor may be treated without parental consent if the situation is serious enough to warrant immediate medical attention. If a minor is a member of an Olympic or World Cup team, the team manager may give consent in the absence of parent or guardian.

Minors also have the right to confidentiality if they give consent. If the minor is legally able to give consent, the doctor cannot tell his or her parents about the disease or treatment. However, minors are told that parents or guardians will obviously learn of the treatment if it goes on their health plans.

Besides minors under certain circumstances and parents or legal guardians, who else can give consent for medical treatment of a minor? Adoptive and divorced parents can do so. If they have joint legal custody, they share the right to make medical decisions. In most cases, the consent of one parent is enough for treatment. However, if there is disagreement between the parents, the decision may go into juvenile court. Unmarried mothers have the legal right for consent. So have natural fathers if there is no question as to paternity. A parent who is himself or herself a minor can make legal decisions for the minor child. Others who can legally give consent are stepparents if they have legally adopted the child or are the legal guardians. Foster parents who are caring for the child by order of the court or by the voluntary wishes of the parent or parents can give consent only to general "ordinary" medical and dental treatment. The parent(s), however, can give written consent for the foster parent to order other types of treatment.

In some areas of health care, neither the parents or children have rights concerning health. Vaccinations are mandatory, for instance, for all children unless a waiver can be obtained. In some cases, neonatal genetic tests are required.

The Right to Health Insurance

Along with defining the medical rights of minors, many states are grappling with how to make sure that all children have the right to health insurance. One of the most

IN 2005, ILLINOIS GOV. ROD R. BLAGOJEVICH SIGNED INTO LAW A
BILL DESIGNED TO GUARANTEE HEALTH INSURANCE TO EVERY CHILD IN
THE STATE.

comprehensive plans was signed into law in Illinois in
late 2005. The expanding coverage will now include the
250,000 uninsured children in the state whose families
include the poor and those earning as much as $40,000
a year.

The program, called All Kids, would, said Governor
Rod R. Blagojevich, "lead the way for a nation that needs
to face a growing problem of middle-income families who
cannot afford insurance premiums." The costs to the family will depend on income. In a family of four with an
income of $41,000 a year, the payment is $40 a month for
one child, or $80 a month for two or more.

The state of Massachusetts went a step further than

Illinois on April 5, 2006. The legislature passed a bill that not only will cover most children in the state but most of the citizens of Massachusetts. All state residents must obtain health coverage by July 1, 2007. Those who can afford it will get tax penalties if they don't buy coverage. Government money given to private insurance plans will fund coverage for the working poor as well as expand the number of children covered. Businesses employing more than ten workers will be fined if they don't provide insurance. This is the first law mandating health insurance in the United States. When it is in full working order, fewer than one percent of the citizens of Massachusetts will be uninsured.

Protecting Mental Health

Sometimes, protecting the medical rights of children involves protecting mental as well as physical health. Just as adults do, children develop psychological problems. According to a survey at the Children's Hospital affiliated with Yale University School of Medicine, hospitals "are admitting many more children with psychiatric emergencies."

The most important step in treating any mental health problem in minors is to recognize the problem in the first place. Ideally, the screening, or initial assessment, is done first by the child's pediatrician. These doctors are not usually specialists in mental disorders, but they are trained to recognize and even treat them. The pediatrician may recommend evaluation by a psychiatrist who specializes in child psychiatry.

The four most common psychiatric disorders in childhood are: depression, unruly or disruptive behavior, anxiety, and attention deficit hyperactivity disorder (ADHD). In his article on these psychiatric disorders, Bruce Tonge says, "Early and timely intervention produces the best chance of a favorable outcome and improves the prognosis for all childhood emotional and behavioral problems."

About 20 percent of adolescents suffer some form of major depression by the time they reach eighteen years of age. More than any other sign, it is a predictor of suicidal behavior in those age fifteen to twenty-four years. Minors react much the same way as adults when they suffer depression. They are persistently sad, sleep little, have little interest in play or friends, and may lose the desire to eat. In addition, the depressed child is also generally irritable and tends to hide bouts of crying. Depression often occurs along with other disorders such as anxiety or ADHD. Contributing factors may be stress in the family or a history of depression. The treatment is usually psychotherapy and family therapy.

Serious patterns of unruly or disruptive behavior occur in boys more than girls and are the most common psychiatric problem in minors.

This form of disturbance often begins in early childhood. The child becomes extremely aggressive and defiant at school and among friends, including animals. Truancy and vandalism are common. Contributing factors may be child abuse, conflict between parents in the home, and poverty or other social disadvantages. Family therapy is usually advised.

The child who suffers from anxiety is most commonly afraid of being separated from home and parents. When that happens, distress symptoms appear, such as shyness, restlessness, headache, stomach pains, nightmares, and an inability to concentrate. Overprotective, anxious parents often contribute to this condition, and family therapy is advised.

According to some surveys, anywhere from 2 to 18 percent of school-age children suffer from ADHD. A survey conducted by the Centers for Disease Control in Atlanta, Georgia, in 2003 indicated that more than four million U.S. children, age four to seventeen, had a history of ADHD diagnosis. More than 50 percent of those diagnosed were being treated with medication. The symptoms include inattention, inability to listen or sit still, excessive talking, and a tendency to be forgetful or disorganized. Treatment includes modifying the environment to reduce distractions, family therapy, and educational programs for learning disabilities.

Explanations of this problem are still controversial. Some experts feel the disorder has a neurobiological basis, and treatment is less successful if the minor also has disruptive behavior problems. Studies show that the child with ADHD does not necessarily grow out of the problem.

The key to management of all these problems of childhood and adolescence is a comprehensive diagnosis and treatment plan. In most cases, drugs still play a limited role, with psychological treatment the most effective.

Suicide

Suicide is the third leading cause of death among adolescents age fifteen to twenty-four, following unintentional injury and homicide. Teens who survive a suicide attempt say they tried to kill themselves because they could not live with a situation that seemed impossible or they felt unbearably sad or depressed. Suicide attempts among teenagers are highest up to about age seventeen or eighteen, probably because older teens have learned to cope with feelings of sadness or intolerable situations.

The warning signs in teenagers who are thinking about suicide include talking about death in general, giving away possessions, talking about feelings of hopelessness, or being unwilling to take part in activities or things that used to be of interest.

There is help for teens, or anyone, thinking of suicide. The suicide crisis line is toll-free and staffed twenty-four hours a day, seven days a week by trained professionals. The calls are confidential. No one who calls has to give up his or her right of privacy.

Rights in the Health-Care System

Step one has been completed; a minor's health-care problem has been diagnosed and treatment suggested. How does the parent navigate the system to pay for the treatment? How does the parent make sure the minor's rights are protected? First, parents should be aware of what expenses are covered for the child in their health-care plans. Next, parents should find out the method by which any insurance decisions may be appealed.

Millions of children in the United States do not have private health care insurance. Two public insurance programs are available to aid children who are not insured: they are Medicaid and CHIP.

Medicaid is a government health-care program for low-income people, including minors. It is run by the states, which receive federal funds for the program and operate under those guidelines. Children in families at or below the poverty line have the right to medical care under this act. Specifics vary from state to state, but all those covered by Medicaid have these rights: to be informed in writing if a benefit is denied; to question a benefit reduction at a special hearing; and to have the use of Medicaid's grievance procedure plan. In addition, if a child receives care under Medicaid and the parents request that the service continue, the child has the right to continued care until the outcome of the hearing.

The other public insurance service is CHIP: Children's Health Insurance Program. It was created in 1997 and is designed for families who cannot afford private health insurance for children but earn too much money for Medicaid. The income range varies by state. Children under this plan are covered by a full range of health services. They include regular checkups, immune shots, prescription drugs, hospital visits, lab tests, and X-rays. Effective in April 2006, CHIP also provides dental services to children under the plan. That includes routine checkups and cleaning, X-rays, and decay prevention techniques.

8
Is Managed Care Manageable?

In the late 1960s, Americans were staggering under the rising costs of health care. Some members of Congress wanted to redo the entire system. New York Governor Nelson A. Rockefeller called for national health insurance. Senator Edward M. Kennedy of Massachusetts introduced a Health Security Bill in early 1970 to insure all Americans.

The final outcome of this rush to remake health care was the Health Maintenance Organization (HMO) Act of 1973. Based on the Kaiser Permanente system in California, it provided money to start similar health-care facilities. There was reason for optimism with the HMO Act because Kaiser's plan was so successful. It was started during World War II for workers in Henry Kaiser's steel mills, shipyards, and other factories. Not aimed at making money, the HMO was designed instead to keep workers healthy. If they stayed healthy, they stayed on the job, thereby helping to build ships, win the war, and make

MODERN-DAY HMOS ARE BASED ON THE MODEL CREATED BY
CALIFORNIA'S KAISER PERMANENTE HOSPITAL SYSTEM JUST AFTER
WWII. HERE, OREGON GOVERNOR CHARLES SPRAGUE AND HENRY
J. AND EDGAR KAISER ACCOMPANY PRESIDENT FRANKLIN DELANO
ROOSEVELT ON A CAMPAIGN TOUR.

money for the company. It worked. As noted by George
Anders in his book *Health Against Wealth*:

> From a base of 30,000 members at the end of
> World War II, Kaiser Permanente grew to
> 250,000 in 1952 and more than one million in the
> 1960s. The Kaiser health plans became known
> as thrifty but reliable, appealing to labor unions
> that wanted to offer full health insurance to their
> workers without paying exorbitant rates. Similar
> group practices started by doctors in other

cities evolved into Health Insurance Plan (HIP) in New York, Group Health Cooperative of Puget Sound in Seattle, and Group Health Association in Washington, D.C.

The HMO Act gives health insurance coverage through doctors, hospitals, and other providers with which the HMO has a contract. The providers usually agree to provide health care at a discount. This allows the HMO to charge lower monthly premiums than other insurers. However, the members have to live with certain restrictions or care guidelines set up by the HMO.

Progress and Reform

When they were set up, say the authors of *Critical Condition: How Health Care in America Became Big Business & Bad Medicine*: "HMOs were expected to create financial incentives for both patients and doctors to avoid elaborate and sometimes unnecessary procedures. To Americans today, the mere mention of HMOs conjures up all that has gone wrong with health care. But years ago, when HMOs were perceived as not-for-profit operations, the view was much more positive. HMOs were seen as way to include more Americans, promote quality care, and hold down costs."

Although HMOs can be organized in many ways, there are four basic models. In the staff model, doctors work for the HMO and have offices in the HMO building. These doctors can see only HMO patients. In the group model, the HMO pays a collection of doctors. The group then distributes the money to the individual doctors. In the independent practice association (IPA), doctors have a contract with the IPA, which has a contract with the HMO. Doctors may work out of their own offices and see HMO and other patients outside the network. In the network model, the HMO has contracts with a combination of groups as well as individual doctors.

Says Anders:

> **Whatever structure was used, most HMOs radically changed the way that physicians and hospitals were paid. No longer did each procedure generate extra income. Instead, many doctors were put on flat monthly rates—a system known as "capitation"—to cover all patient care, no matter how healthy or sick the plan member was.**

Hospitals also had fixed payment rates, especially for treating specific illnesses. The less time spent in the hospital, the fewer expenditures for the medical providers.

When Bill Clinton became president in 1993, one of his priorities was health-care reform. He had made it a campaign promise, and once in office he set up a health-care task force headed by Hillary Clinton.

It was called "Hillary Care" by some detractors. The plan proposed changes in funding and asked the government to pay insurers if they took on extra costs when accepting high-risk patients. Congress vetoed the whole idea and instead, along with state legislatures, passed many piecemeal laws that tried to reduce costs to the public.

How Managed Care Works

Although HMOs are the most recognizable and the oldest form of managed care, in fact, most health care is managed care today. Almost no one can afford the costs of private health care. Another popular health-care plan is the PPO—preferred provider organization. The PPO makes arrangements with doctors, hospitals, and other medical providers who agree to offer services at a reduced rate. That makes cost sharing lower within the network.

IN **1998, PRESIDENT BILL CLINTON** SPOKE AT A RALLY IN FAVOR OF A "PATIENTS' BILL OF RIGHTS" THAT WOULD GUARANTEE RIGHTS SUCH AS A CHOICE OF MEDICAL PROVIDERS AND PARTICIPATION IN TREATMENT PLANS.

When you are out of school and ready for a full-time job, you will probably have the opportunity to join an HMO or other health care plan. Since an informed consumer is generally the best—and happiest—consumer, you should first understand how these plans work and what they offer you. HMOs are described here, but most plans work along similar lines.

The idea of health plans is that by taking care of your health at present, you can avoid medical problems down the line. In an HMO, you can usually get wider coverage for less money than through a traditional insurance company. However, unlike traditional insurance, you usually must use the HMO's medical providers.

You do not always have broad freedom of choice with an HMO. Some may operate only within certain areas, called "service areas." You must be within that area to receive medical treatment. In some cases, you might not be able to be treated by your usual family physician, if you have one. You might have to choose your doctor, called a primary care physician (PCP), from a list of those employed by the HMO, that is, those within its network. In addition, all your medical care—from doctors, hospitals, and pharmacies—will come from within that network. Your PCP will be in charge of your medical needs and will refer you to specialists if needed. Women can also choose a principal health-care provider (WPHCP), an obstetrician or gynecologist in the network. If the HMO offers a prescription drug plan, it may choose which drugs your doctors can prescribe, perhaps ruling out expensive drugs.

You can see that joining an HMO is a tradeoff. The lower costs may allow you to carry health insurance but your choices about your care are limited.

What if you simply don't like the PCP you selected from the HMO's network? In most cases, the HMO allows you to choose another one, up to four times a year.

Health Care Plans

You've started a new job and are offered a health-care plan. You may not have a choice in the company's plan, but you should be familiar with its services. With an HMO, for instance, look at its service record to customers. Complaints filed against a health-care provider are a good indication of its service. Complaints can be viewed from Web sites such as the National Committee for Quality Assurance (www.ncqa.org). It is an independent monitoring organization that issues report cards to HMOs. There also may be a consumer help line resource in your area.

Payments

How do you pay for managed care? If you are employed, your health-care costs are taken out of your paycheck. In addition, every time you visit a doctor or get medical care, you will owe a copayment. The HMOs pay 100 percent to cover all services from their network providers in excess of the copayment. Therefore, if you pay a $20 copayment for an office visit and the rate according to contract for the doctor is $70, the HMO will pay the doctor $50.

Patients' Rights

State laws differ in their protection of patients' rights in HMOs and other plans. The state of Texas has some of the strictest patient protection laws in the country. They include requiring the HMO to have a procedure that allows members to protest any of its decisions, such as if the HMO denies a certain recommended medical treatment. If the matter is not resolved to the member's satisfaction, he or she can ask for a review by the Independent Review Organization (IRO). That decision is binding.

The HMO in Texas must have a method to resolve member complaints. If a member or doctor files a complaint, the HMO cannot "fire" the member or doctor. The

DEBORAH MORAN TOOK HER SEVEN-YEAR LEGAL BATTLE WITH HER INSURER TO THE SUPREME COURT TO LET THEM DECIDE WHETHER HMO PATIENTS ARE ENTITLED TO OUTSIDE REVIEW. ON JUNE 22, 2002, THE COURT SIDED WITH MORAN.

U.S. Health Care System: Not a Pretty Picture

According to John Rother, policy director of AARP (American Association of Retired Persons), the U.S. health-care system is not in good shape. He blames the fall on three factors:

1. There are too many insurers in the system today, each fighting for profits. In the mid-twentieth century, there was only Blue Cross. Also, the single-family doctor has all but disappeared. Today, a patient will often have to see two or more doctors to diagnose or treat an illness.

2. There is a decline in the number of employers today who offer health insurance. About 46 million Americans are currently uninsured.

3. The costs of health care are constantly on the rise.

Rother says reorganization is needed so that the whole system works more efficiently. He also thinks that every American concerned with health care must join in the cry for better treatment.

HMO cannot stop doctors from discussing your medical options, even if that means filing a complaint against the HMO itself. Other rights include access to adequate medical facilities within a certain mileage and referral to specialists for life-threatening, chronic, or disabling illnesses.

In New York State in 2003, a federal appeals court of the second circuit expanded the rights of patients to sue HMOs. It said that HMOs could be sued for malpractice for injuries that resulted from refusal to allow a medically necessary treatment. Such claims had been rejected by courts in the past. After the ruling, David L. Trueman, one of the lawyers who filed the suit, said: "This ruling means that there's now no barrier for anyone in New York, Connecticut or Vermont to sue an H.M.O. when the health plan denies treatment recommended by a doctor. Millions of consumers have a right they did not have before."

The decision came from *Cicio* v. *Vytra Healthcare*. In 1998, the oncologist for Carmine Cicio of Suffolk County, New York, requested Vytra's approval to treat him with high-dose chemotherapy and his own stem cells. Cicio suffered from a blood cancer called multiple myeloma. But Vytra's medical director denied the request, saying the procedure was experimental. The company approved a different treatment, and Cicio died that May. Many experts felt that even though the ruling applied only to New York, Connecticut, and Vermont, the area covered by the second circuit court, it would likely be an influence elsewhere.

Since their inception, there have been complaints against HMOs, mostly, it is believed, in the area of refusing treatment. However, a study that looked at more than 1,700 appeals between 1998 and mid–2000 by patients in two large health plans in California had some interesting results. Only 37 percent of the cases concerned whether a service or treatment was denied. Of the 37 percent, a little more than half were decided in the patient's favor. Most of the other appeals questioned whether the service was covered by the contract of the HMO or whether the patient had the right to services outside the HMO network. Most of those were decided in favor of the HMO.

The study indicates that most people do not have complaints about HMO services, and the complaints they do have are relatively minor. In fact, HMOs—with their benefits and faults—are about the only really affordable health care that exists. If they have power over consumers, so do insurance companies that finance health-care plans. What they allow in services raises the same issues as do HMOs. You may not have a choice of medical benefits, but you do have the choice of knowing what you're paying for.

Epilogue:
Navigating the
Medical System

No matter what your age, it is never too early to learn how to navigate the medical system. You are already part of it. You were probably born in a hospital. You have been vaccinated and have had doctor checkups. You might have been a hospital patient for a broken leg or bad case of the flu. The U.S. medical system is one of the world's best. But it helps at any age to know the ropes.

Becoming part of the medical system by entering a hospital, for instance, is, according to a 2005 *New York Times* article, "often degrading. [At many hospitals] small courtesies that help lubricate and dignify civil society are neglected precisely when they are needed most, when people are feeling acutely cut off from others and betrayed by their own bodies."

In this atmosphere, says the article, otherwise reasonable patients become afraid of those who are supposed to be caring for them. They rarely file formal complaints when something is wrong, even though that is their right.

They are often reluctant to call a patient representative to complain. The Society for Healthcare Consumer Advocacy, an association of patient representatives formed in 1972, wants patients to be encouraged to speak up. It's the best way to get their complaints heard.

The care of an elderly and well-known woman, Brooke Astor, became news during the summer of 2006. A wealthy philanthropist, at the age of 104, she was being cared for at home. But her grandson charged that she was being mistreated, not fed or cared for properly. Her son, who has financial charge of her affairs, denied the accusation. However, the court at least temporarily removed the son as her financial advocate.

Patient representatives often urge those entering a hospital, especially for a serious procedure, to first fill out an advance medical directive. That will let both doctors and family members know exactly what to do in case the patient is unable to speak for himself or herself.

The onset of illness is confusing and frightening for most people, especially for the millions of Americans who live alone without family members nearby. Even those with caring family members generally need help in navigating the medical system. To aid all of them, organizations such as CancerCare offer help with medical information.

Sometimes the anxiety over the medical system is simply a result of too much information. We are awash in data every day, from television, radio, and computers. Where can the patient turn when there is too much to digest? A 2005 article in the *New York Times* told of the medical dilemma of Meg Gaines of Wisconsin, age thirty-nine and the mother of two young children. She had inoperable ovarian cancer. After treatments in cancer centers in California and Texas, she returned home not knowing where to find further help. Three of her medical oncologists told her to stick with the latest chemotherapy, which seemed to be working. But two others advised a new procedure—surgery and chemotherapy, which they believed would be more effective. Meg asked one of the doctors, "Who will decide?" He replied: "We're in the outer regions of medical knowledge, and none of us knows what you should do. So you have to make the decision, based on your values." She replied, "I'm not a doctor! I'm a criminal defense lawyer! How am I supposed to know!"

Like Meg, many people today are faced with the right—as well as the burden—to choose among the many treatment options that may be offered. If Meg had faced the same cancer years earlier, her primary doctor would probably have offered one treatment and she would have complied. But today there are so many options that even her primary doctor would not be familiar with or competent to judge.

What is the best way to navigate the medical system? Most medical workers say, first, become the most informed consumer possible. Know your rights and know your options. That is what Meg Gaines did in 1995 when she was forced with a decision. She chose the newer treatment, surgery plus chemotherapy. And she seems to have made the right choice. In 2001, she helped to found the Center for Patient Partnerships at the law school of the University of Wisconsin at Madison. The center assists those with cancer and other diseases to locate the right doctors and get enough information to help them make intelligent decisions.

Another area where patients' rights are blurred is the workplace. What happens if you have an illness that might prevent you from doing your job? Do you have the right to take off extra time for tests or therapy? Rather than face that problem, many people in such situations keep the illness a secret as long as possible. Afraid to lose their jobs, they are aware that the first concern of employers, no matter how sympathetic, is running the business, not tending to the workers.

Yet, even if you want to remain silent, talking about the illness is the way to get help. The Americans with Disabilities Act, passed in 1990, demands that employers make reasonable concessions to accommodate workers with illness or disability. That applies as long as the worker can do the essential work required on the job. For instance, a disability might limit how long a worker can stand. But if he is able to perform the tasks while sitting down, then the law says he is doing the essential work. As for time off for hospital visits or treatment, the Family and Medical Leave Act (1993) allows up to three months off from work without losing the job or health insurance.

Workers at small companies face an added threat, since the Family and Medical Leave Act applies only to those places that employ fifty or more. And in this time of rising insurance costs, even those companies that are covered by law may make personnel decisions based on health-care costs. For instance, Wal-Mart, the giant retailer, experienced a 15 percent increase in health-care costs in 2004. An internal memorandum that was leaked to the press said that the company could save millions of dollars a year if it did not hire people with health problems. How could Wal-Mart *not* hire such people? According to the memo, the idea was to make sure every job also entailed some sort of physical activity. For instance, say the ad called for a cashier in the sporting goods department, which ordinarily entails mostly sitting at the register. The new job description would add something like: Must also on occasion climb ladders to stock new sports equipment. Someone with leg or back problems or who was obese would not, under that description, be hired.

Illness, whether in school or on the job, can be a frightening experience. Getting help for an illness often puts a person in a vulnerable place. But knowledge of your rights and responsibilities in that place can ease some of the fears and give you confidence. Confidence, in turn, can provide a measure of control that helps to navigate the often complicated world that is the medical system.

Notes

Chapter 1

p. 16, par. 2, Kermit L. Hall, ed., *The Oxford Companion to the Supreme Court of the United States*. New York: Oxford University Press, 1992, pp. 209–210.

p. 18, par. 1, Timothy E. Quill,, M.D. "Terri Schiavo—A Tragedy Compounded," *The New England Journal of Medicine*, 352:1630–1633 (April 21, 2005): 1.

p. 21, par 5, Abby Goodnough, "Schiavo Autopsy Says Brain, Withered, Was Untreatable," *New York Times*, June 15, 2005, p. A1.

p. 22, pars. 1–2, Ibid.

p. 22, pars. 3–4, Fr. John T. Zuhlsdorf, "Outlines Care of Persons in 'Persistent Vegetative State," *Wanderer Newspaper*, www.thewanderpess.com (Accessed June 5, 2005).

p. 22, par. 5, Barbara Kralis, "Catholics Supporting the Denial of 'Nutrition and Hydration' are not in Communion with the Church," *Catholic Online*, www.catholic.org/printer_friendly, (Accessed May 3, 2005).

Chapter 2

p. 28, par. 2, "Jack Kevorkian," *Current Biography*, H. W. Wilson, 1994, p. 2.

p. 28, par.3, Ibid.

p. 30, par. 3, Wesley J. Smith, "A 'Dr Death' Runs for President," *National Review*, September 4, 2003: 1.

p. 31, par. 4–p. 32, par. 1, Hugh Hewitt, "Death by Committee," www.weeklystandard.com/Content/Public/Articles Accessed January 18, 2006).

p. 32, pars. 2–3, "The Groningen Protocol," www.another think.com/contents/postmodern_culture/20041203_the_groningen_prot (Accessed January 18, 2006).

Chapter 3

p. 35, par. 2–p. 36, par. 1, Julie Cantor, and Ken Baum, "The Limits of Conscientious Objection—May Pharmacists Refuse to Fill Prescriptions for Emergency Contraception?" *New England Journal of Medicine*, 351: 2008–2012, November 4, 2004.

p 38, par. 4–p. 39, par. 1, Jeanne Kassler, *Bitter Medicine: Greed and Chaos in American Health Care*. New York: Birch Lane, 1994, p. 93.

p. 40, par. 2–p. 43, par. 1, "Vioxx Recalled By Merck Worldwide," http//arthritis.about.com/old/vioxx/a/vioxxrecall.htm(Accessed March 15, 2006).

p. 48, par. 3, Steven Reinberg, "U.S. Preemie Births, Caesareans Reach Record Highs," *Healthfinder*, November 15, 2005, pp. 1–2.

Chapter 4

p. 53, par. 3, Denise Grady, "Trying to Avoid 2nd Caesarean, Many Find Choice Isn't Theirs," *New York Times*, November 29, 2004, p. A1.

p. 54, par. 3, Robert F. Borenstein, and Mary A. Languirand, *When Someone You Love Needs Nursing Home Care*. New York: Newmarket Press, 2001, p. 16.

p. 57, par. 2, "Colonscopy Far More Cost-effective against Colon Cancer than promising Cox II drugs, study predicts," www.eurekalert.org/pub_releases/2003-5/vomhcfm 050103.php, (Accessed March 17, 2006).

p. 59, par. 2, Abigail Zuger, "For a Retainer, Lavish Care by 'Boutique Doctors,'" *New York Times*, October 30, 2005, p. 26.

p. 60, par. 1, Jo Kaufman, "Boutique Doctors," *Nob Hill Gazette*, January 2004, p.4.

p. 60, par. 3, Zuger, "For a Retainer," p. 26.

p. 60, par. 4, Carole Fleck, "Want Your Doctor to Pamper You? Pay Extra," *AARP Bulletin*, March 16, 2006.

Chapter 5

p. 67, pars. 3–4, Melvin I. Urofsky, *Letting Go: Death, Dying & the Law*. New York: Scribners, 1993, p. 8.

p. 70, par. 4. George J. Annas, *The Rights of Patients*. Totowa, NJ: Humana, 1992, p. 178.

p. 72, par. 6–p. 73, part. 1, "Protecting the Privacy of Patients' Health Information," U.S. Department of Health & Human Services Fact Sheet, p. 10, April 14, 2003.

p. 81, par. 1, Gina Kolata, "Making the Most of a Brief Office Visit," *New York Times*, November 30, 2005, p. A28.

Chapter 6

p. 85, par. 2,"*Roe v. Wade*," http//en.wikipedia.org/wiki/Roe_v._Wade, (Accessed March 21, 2006).

p. 85, par. 2, Kermit L. Hall, ed., *The Oxford Companion to the Supreme Court of the United States*. New York: Oxford University Press, p. 74.

p. 89, par. 2, The Pregnant Patient's Bill of Rights, p. 1, www.aimsusa.org/ppbr.htm (Accessed March 25, 2006).

p. 90, par. 2, Father Mark Hodges, "Destructive Embryonic Stem Cell Research," www.antiochian.org/stem-cell-research (Accessed March 15, 2006).

p. 93, par. 2, "Proposition 71," www.smartvoter.org/2004/11/02/ca/state/prop/71 (Accessed April 4, 2006).

p. 94, par. 2, Richard M. Doerflinger, "What Does the Cloning Scandal Mean?" www.usccb.org/prolife/publicat/lifeissues/011306.htm, (Accessed March 25, 2006).

p. 96, par. 1, Mike Hendriks, "The Debate over Stem Cell Research," *McCook Daily Gazette* (Accessed October 29, 2004).

Chapter 7

p. 97, par. 2–p. 98, par. 1, "Hodgkin's Returns to Girl Whose Parents Fought State," *New York Times*, June 11, 2005, p.A8.

p. 98, par. 2, "Hodgkins Returns," p. A8.

p. 103, par. 2, "Illinois Law Offers Coverage for Uninsured Children," *New York Times*, November 16, 2005.

p. 104, par. 2, "Childhood Psychiatric Emergencies Rising," *Nursing*, September 2000.

p. 104, par. 4–p. 105, par. 1, "Common Child and Adolescent Psychiatric Problems and Their Management in the Community,

www.mja.com.au/public/mentalhealth/articles/tonge/tonge
.html (Accessed April 5, 2006).

Chapter 8

p. 110, par. 1–p. 111, p. 1, George Anders, *Health Against Wealth*. Boston: Houghton Mifflin, 1996, p. 26.

p.111, par. 3, Donald L. Barlett, and James B. Steele, *Critical Condition: How Health Care in America Became Big Business & Bad Medicine*. New York: Doubleday, 2004, p. 89.

p. 112, par. 2, Anders, *Health*, p. 27.

p. 118, par. 3, Robert Pear, "A Court Expands the Rights Of Patients to Sue HMOs," *New York Times*, February 18, 2003, p. A8.

Epilogue

p. 120, par. 2, Benedict Carey, "In the Hospital, a Degrading Shift from Person to Patient," *New York Times*, August 16, 2005, p. A1.

p. 121, par. 3, Jan Hoffman, "Awash in Information, Patients Face Lonely, Uncertain Road," *New York Times*, August 14, 2005, p. A1.

Further Information

Caregiver Organizations

CancerCare 800-813-4673

Family Caregiver Alliance 800-445-8106

National Family Caregivers Association 800-896-3650

Sharecancersupport 866-891-2392

Suicide crisis line 800-SUICIDE or 800-999-9999

Web Sites

Familiesusa.org
Watchdog for children's health care

Health.nih.gov
General consumer health data

Teenhealthfx.com
Information on teen health problems

Teen-Pregnancy.Info
www.teen-pregnancy.info
Answers questions about teen pregnancy

Bibliography

Books

Anders, George. *Health Against Wealth*. Boston: Houghton Mifflin, 1996.

Annas, George J. *The Rights of Patients*. Totowa, NJ: Humana, 1992.

Barron, Bruce A., M.D. *Outsmarting Managed Care*. New York: Times Books, 1999.

Barlett, Donald L., and James B. Steele. *Critical Condition: How Health Care in America Became Big Business & Bad Medicine*. New York: Doubleday, 2004.

Borenstein, Robert F., and Mary A. Languirand. *When Someone You Love Needs Nursing Home Care*. New York: Newmarket Press, 2001.

Coombs, Jan Gregoire. *The Rise and Fall of HMOs*. Madison: University of Wisconsin Press, 2005.

Dauner, C. Duane, with Michael Bowker. *The Health Care Solution*. Sacramento, CA: Vision, 1994.

Faraone, Stephen V. *Straight Talk about Your Child's Mental Health*. New York: Guilford, 2003.

Hall, Kermit L. ed. *The Oxford Companion to the Supreme Court of the United States.* New York: Oxford University Press, 1992, pp. 209–210.

Hombs, Mary Ellen. *Welfare Reform.* Santa Barbara,CA: ABC-CLIO, 1996.

Kassler, Jeanne, M.D. *Bitter Medicine: Greed and Chaos in American Health Care.* New York: Birch Lane Press, 1994.

Koenig, Harold G., and Douglas M. Lawson. *Faith in the Future: Health Care, Aging, and the Role of Religion.* Philadelphia: Templeton Foundation, 2004.

Millenson, Michael L. *Demanding Medical Excellence.* Chicago: University of Chicago Press, 1997.

Quill, Timothy E. *Death and Dignity: Making Choices and Taking Charge.* New York: Norton, 1993.

Rubenstein, William B., Ruth Eisenberg, and Lawrence O. Gostin. *The Rights of People Who Are HIV Positive.* Carbondale: Southern Illinois University Press, 1996.

Urofsky, Melvin I. *Letting Go: Death, Dying & the Law.* New York: Scribner's, 1993.

Wurtele, Sandy K., and Cindy L. Miller-Perrin. *Preventing Child Sexual Abuse.* Lincoln: University of Nebraska Press, 1992.

Zgola, Jitka M. *Care That Works: A Relationship Approach to Persons with Dementia.* Baltimore: Johns Hopkins University Press, 1999.

Articles

Abrey, Julia. "Private Client/Family: A Matter of Life and Death," *Lawyer*, March 27, 2005.

Ackerman, Todd. "Study: Shorter rehab stays may put patients in danger," *Houston Chronicle*, October 13, 2004.

Anglin, Maria. "Moral meddling is bad medicine," *San Antonio Express-News*, May 2, 2005.

Cantor, Julie, and Ken Baum, "The Limits of Conscientious Objection—May Pharmacists Refuse to Fill Prescriptions for Emergency Contraception?" *New England Journal of Medicine*, 351:2008-2012 (November 4, 2004).

"Childhood Psychiatric Emergencies Rising," *Nursing*, September 2000.

Chevlen, Eric. "Free to Die," *First Things*, August/September 1999, 95:18–20.

Carey, Benedict. "In the Hospital, a Degrading Shift from Person to Patient," *New York Times*, August 16, 2005, pp. A11–12.

"Essential but Uncommon Knowledge: Patients Have Many Rights, Just Ask," *New York Times*, August 16, 2005, p. A1.

Fleck, Carole, "Want Your Doctor to Pamper You?" *AARP Bulletin*, October 2004, pp. 1–2.

————. "Want Your Doctor to Pamper You? Pay Extra," *AARP Bulletin*, March 16, 2006. p. 2.

Getlin, Josh. "The Death of Terri Schiavo," *Los Angeles Times*, April 1, 2005, p. 1.

Goodnough, Abby. "Schiavo Autopsy Says Brain, Withered, Was Untreatable," *New York Times*, June 15, 2005, p. A1.

Grady, Denise, "Trying to Avoid 2nd Caesarean, Many Find Choice Isn't Theirs," *New York Times*, November 29, 2004, p. A1.

Harmon, Amy. "How About Not 'Curing' Us, Some Autistics Are Pleading," *New York Times*, December 20, 2004, p. A1.

Hendriks, Mike. "The Debate over Stem Cell Research," *McCook Daily Gazette*, October 29, 2004, p. 1.

"Hodgkin's Returns to Girl Whose Parents Fought State," *New York Times*, June 11, 2005, p. A8.

"Illinois Law Offers Coverage for Uninsured Children," *New York Times*, November 16, 2005, p. A1.

Hoffman, Jan. "Awash in Information, Patients Face a Lonely, Uncertain Road, *New York Times*, August 14, 2005, p. A1.

Kaufman, Jo. "Boutique Doctors: Customized Care," *Nob Hill Gazette*, January 2006, p. 4.

Kolata, Gina. "Making the Most of a Brief Office Visit," *New York Times*, November 30, 2005, p. A28.

Kornblut, Anne E. "A Next Step: Making Rules To Die By," *New York Times*, April 1, 2005, p. A1.

Kuntzman, Gersh. "American Beat: A Living Will," *Newsweek*, March 28, 2005, pp. 1–2.

Pear, Robert. "A Court Expands the Rights of Patients to Sue HMOs," *New York Times*, February 18, 2003, p. A8.

Reynolds, Maura. "After Schiavo, GOP's Push on End-of-Life Issues Fades," *Los Angeles Times*, April 7, 2005, p. 3.

Simon, Richard, and Janet Hook. "The Terri Schiavo Case," *Los Angeles Times*, March 25, 2005, p. 10.

Smith, Wesley J. "A 'Dr Death' Runs for President," *National Review*, September 4, 2003, p. 1.

Tansey, Bernadette. "Hard Sell: How Marketing Drives the Pharmaceutical Industry," *San Francisco Chronicle*, May 6, 2005, p. 1.

Quill, Timonthy E. "Terri Schiavo-A Tragedy Compounded," *New England Journal of Medicine*, April 21, 2005, 352: 1630 –1633.

Tolle, Susan. "A Study in What Not to Do," *Modern Health-care*, April 4, 2005, pp. 1–2.

Tolson, Jay. "Wrestling with the Final Call," *U.S. News & World Report*, April 4, 2005.

Zuger, Abigail. "For a Retainer Lavish Care by 'Boutique Doctors,'" *New York Times*, October 30, 2005, p. A1.

Web Sites

"Colonoscopy Far More Cost-effective against Colon Cancer than Promising Cox II Drugs, Study Predicts," www.eurekalert.org/pub_releases/2003-05 (Accessed March 17, 2006).

"Common Child and Adolescent Psychiatric Problems and their Management in the Community," www.mja.com.au/public/mentalhealth/articles/tonge/tonge.html (Accessed April 3, 2006).

Doerflinger, Richard M. "What Does the Cloning Scandal Mean?" www.usccb.org/prolife/publicat/lifeissues/0ll306.htm (Accessed March 25, 2006).

"The Groningen Protocol," www.anotherthink.com/contents/postmodern_culture/20041203_the_groningen_prot (Accessed January 18, 2006).

Hewitt, Hugh, "Death by Committee," www.weeklystandard/com/Content/Public/Articles (Accessed January 18, 2006).

Hodges, Father Mark, "Destructive Embryonic Stem Cell Research," www.antiochian.org/stem-cell-research (Accessed March 15, 2006).

"HMOs to Us: So What Are You All Complaining About?" www.yourdoctorinthefamily.com/commentary/comm066.htm (Accessed February 13, 2006).

"How HMO's Work," www.healthinsure.com/hmo_plans .html (Accessed February 25, 2006).

Kowalczyk, Liz. "Rising Doctors' Premiums Not Due to Lawsuit Awards," www.boston.com/business/globe/articles (Accessed March 14, 2006).

Kralis, Barbara. "Catholics Supporting the Denial of 'Nutrition and Hydration' Are Not in Communion with the Church," *Catholic Online*, www.catholic.org/printer_friendly (Accessed May 3, 2005).

"Medical cannabis."en.wikipedia.org/wiki/Medical_marijuana (Accessed February 21, 2006).

"Patient's Bill of Rights," www.library.dal.ca/kellogg/Bioethics /codes/rights.htm (Accessed March 15, 2006).

"The Pregnant Patient's Bill of Rights," www.aimsusa.org/ ppbr.htm (Accessed March 25, 2006).

"Proposition 71," www.smartvoter.org/2004/11/02/ca/state/ prop/71 (Accessed April 4, 2006).

Records of the Department of Children and Family Services, www.miami.edu./ethics/schiavo (Accessed April 4, 2006).

Reinberg, Steven. "U.S. Preemie Births, Caesareans Reach Record Highs," *Healthfinder*, November 15, 2005, pp. 1–2.

"*Roe* v. *Wade*," (http)//en.wikipedia.org/wiki/Roe_v._Wade (Accessed March 21, 2006).

U.S. Department of Health & Human Services Fact Sheet, www.hhs.gov/news/facts/privacy (Accessed April 14, 2003).

"Vioxx Recalled by Merck Worldwide," (http)//arthritis.about. com/od/vioxx/a/vioxxrecall.htm (Accessed March 15, 2006).

Zuhlsdorf, John T. "Outlines Care of Persons in 'Persistent Vegetative State.'" *The Wanderer*, www.thewanderpress.com (Accessed June 5, 2005).

Index

Page numbers in **boldface** are illustrations, tables, and charts.

About the Author

A former U.S. Navy journalist and children's book editor, **Corinne J. Naden** lives in Tarrytown, New York. She is the author of more than ninety nonfiction books for young readers. Her most recent book for Marshall Cavendish was *Dred Scott: Person or Property?* in our Supreme Court Milestones series.